THE ILLUMINATED
Book of Days

At Christmas I no more desire a rose
Than wish a snow in May's new-fangled mirth;
But like of each thing that in season grows.

Shakespeare, Love's Labours Lost

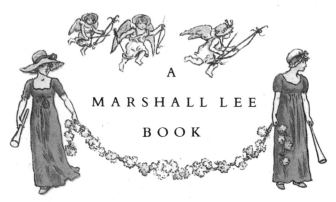

A
MARSHALL LEE
BOOK

G. P. Putnam's Sons

NEW YORK

THE ILLUMINATED
Book of Days

EDITED BY
KAY & MARSHALL LEE

WITH ILLUSTRATIONS BY
KATE GREENAWAY
AND
Eugène Grasset

Library of Congress Cataloguing in Publication data
Main entry under title:
The Illuminated book of days.
"A Marshall Lee book."
1. Almanacs, American. 2. Handbooks, vade-
mecums, etc. I. Lee,Kay. II. Lee, Marshall.
AY71 1979 051 79-87621
ISBN 0-399-12406-3

Printed in the United States of America

PROLOGUE

In the time when travel across the ocean was done in ships, it was the custom to give the departing traveller a "steamer basket" to help fill the long days at sea. These shamelessly tempting collections of fresh and candied fruits, assorted nuts, and exotic delicacies put no constraints of order or limit on their happy new owners—they were there to be sampled when and how the impulse flowed. So it is with *The Illuminated Book of Days*, a treasury of delights to take on your voyage through the year.

This book has for ancestors a spate of Books of Days published in the 19th century in England, the most famous of which is the massive two-volume work by Chambers. Its cousins are the almanacs and farming manuals that guided people through the years from Elizabethan times to the present. Its early ancestors are the medieval Books of Hours—which were also illuminated with beautiful pictures in color.

In the sense that this book of days is a calendar, it is a perpetual one—good for any and all years. A partial exception is in the dating of the movable feasts. Most ancient festivals occur at times related to the phases of the moon or to a combination of lunar and solar activity, so these are celebrated on different days each year according to our own calendar, which is based on the sun. For simplicity's sake, the dates of such events are given in *The Illuminated Book of Days* for the year beginning March 1, 1980 and ending on February 28, 1981. For good measure, we have included a February 29th, even though leap year falls in 1980.

Speaking of dates, there have been several changes in the solar calendar since it was adopted, so many occurrences could be attributed correctly to two or more dates—depending on whether the calendar of the time or the present calendar is used. This, needless to say, can become extremely confusing. In 46 B.C. Julius Caesar adopted the Julian calendar, which was used generally in the Western world until 1582, when Pope Gregory promulgated the "New Style" calendar that moved everything forward by eleven days. This was immediately adopted by Roman Catholic countries, but did not become official in the British Empire—which then included the American colonies—until 1752. Russia and China held out until the early 20th century and each experimented for some years with still other systems. On top of all this is the confusion caused by the international date line—which puts an occurrence in one day on one side of the line and the next, or previous, day on the other side. So it is quite possible that the reader will see elsewhere dates that disagree with those in this book, which are the dates found by the editors in the most respected reference sources. The chances are that *both* dates will be "correct", as such matters go.

Few people today realize that before the New Style calendar was adopted, the year began in March. For all the thousands of years of man, a year was the lifetime of nature, the inevitable process of conception, birth, flowering, death, and decay: spring, summer, autumn, winter. Until only two hundred and some years ago in the English-speaking world, law followed nature. Indeed, New Year's Day is still March 21st—the time of the spring equinox—in Iran and other parts of the Middle East. In Europe and North America, farm life inevitably begins in spring and winds down in winter—celebrating the "New Year" halfway through the intermission at the end of its cycle. *The Illuminated Book of Days* goes along with nature and begins the year in the old way—with March.

The Illuminated Book of Days is published for your pleasure and information. However, it is not an encyclopedia. While the editors have checked the facts in the text as far as seemed reasonable, the "facts" of folklore and old literature are elusive and often indistinct. It is not uncommon to find different versions of an early custom in two or more "authoritative" sources. Even the present customs of a country may be practiced in one part but be unknown or different in another. We have sifted what we found and have provided what we believe to be the most accurate information available.

Many text entries are pieces of verse or prose that range in date from the Middle Ages to the mid-19th century, and are either anonymous or the work of forgotten writers. Some of these items come from the farming almanacs of Thomas Tusser and his contemporaries in the 16th century and can be recognized by their charmingly archaic language and spelling. Other entries—particularly recipes and household hints—come from the numerous housekeeping books of the 18th and 19th centuries, such as those of Mrs. Beeton and Mrs. Rundell. Author's names are given only when the writer has present literary or historical interest.

The illustrations, on the other hand, are from only one period—the last three decades of the Victorian era. Except for the large plates that begin the months—which are the work of Eugène Grasset, who, with Toulouse-Lautrec, originated the French art nouveau poster style—all of the color illustrations are by Kate Greenaway. Perhaps the most popular children's book illustrator of all time, Kate Greenaway also illustrated books for adults—notably the lovely *Language of Flowers* and the fourteen annual Almanacs. Illustrations from all of these tiny, delightful gems are represented in the following pages. The reproductions of all the color illustrations have been made from first editions of the original works. The small pen drawings that illustrate the text are also by K.G. They have been reproduced from an original edition of the artist's famous *Birthday Book*. The other black-and-white illustrations are engravings from books of the same period. Like much of the text material, these pictures are anonymous.

We should like to acknowledge and express our gratitude to the people who helped us with the research that made *The Illuminated Book of Days* possible: Virginia Kelley, Peter Lee, Alex Hand, Stephen Paul Davis, Harry de Winter, Justin Schiller, Katharine Gregory, Jo Ann Reisler, and Doris Frohnsdorf.

K L / M L

March.

1	Saturday	17	Monday
2	2 S. IN LENT	18	Tuesday
3	Monday	19	Wednesday
4	Tuesday	20	Thursday
5	Wednesday	21	Friday
6	Thursday	22	Saturday
7	Friday	23	5 S. IN LENT
8	Saturday	24	Monday
9	3 S. IN LENT	25	ANNUNCIA.
10	Monday	26	Wednesday
11	Tuesday	27	Thursday
12	Wednesday	28	Friday
13	Thursday	29	Saturday
14	Friday	30	PALM SUN.
15	Saturday	31	Monday
16	4 S. IN LENT		

Whan that month in which the world bigan,
That highte March, whan God first maked man.

Chaucer

March was the beginning of the legal
year in Great Britain and the Colonies
until 1752. Thus, for example, from
February 24, 1710, to March 4, 1711,
was 8 days, not a year and 8 days.

1

In the ancient Roman calendar, this day was the feast of the Matronalia, when patrician women held feasts for their slaves.

Frederic Chopin born, 1810.
"Hats off, gentlemen—a genius!"
Robert Schumann

George Washington's way of curing colds was to eat a toasted onion before going to bed.

A dry March and a dry May portend a wholesome summer, if there be a showering April between.

Francis Bacon

St. David, the patron saint of Wales, died in 601. On St. David's Day, Welsh people wear leeks in their hats. According to legend, St. David instructed Welsh soldiers to wear leeks in their hats in a battle against the Saxons, so they could distinguish their own troops from the enemy's.

On the first of any month, British schoolchildren believe that before speaking to anyone else you must say "white rabbits" for luck. Some say "hares and rabbits" or just "rabbits".

2

The first ballet is performed in London in 1717.

PURIM

Purim commemorates the day when the beautiful Jewish Queen Esther saved the Jews of Persia from destruction by Haman, the chief minister of King Ahasuerus and enemy of the Jews. At Esther's behest Haman was hanged by the King instead of the Jews being hanged by Haman. ("To hang as high as Haman" is a popular expression.) At Purim pageants, where exaggerated parodies of the story are acted out, a pretty girl is chosen to play Queen Esther, and everyone brings noisemakers to drown out the name of the wicked Haman. A Purim treat is *Hamantashan* —pastries filled with poppyseed or prunes (their name means "Haman's ear!")

Leaping has always been part of the rites to encourage crops to grow high. Mars, for whom March is named, was a Roman god of the crops as well as the war god. He had young warrior-priests called Salii, or "leapers", who spent the month of March in leaping processions all over Italy.

"Mad as a March hare" is an old saying. Hares are unusually shy and wild in March, which is their rutting season.

3

In 1895 Munich begins to give a driving test for bicycle riders. Those who pass receive license plates for their bicycles.

In 1884 a Munich businessman and his wife rode a home made bicycle down the main street. A headline in a leading newspaper protested the next day: "A SCANDELOUS DRIVE" "Without shame, proud as an Amazon, this fine lady let herself be inspected by one and all. Shall propriety be dealt such a blow with impunity?"

Doll Festival in Japan. Also called Peach Blossom Festival since, to the Japanese, that flower symbolizes the little girls whose dolls are honored on this day. Their dolls are on display, but this is really the big day for little girls.

4

As many mists as ye have in March, so many frosts in July.

March.

1|Thursday.	12|Monday.	22|Thursday.
2|Friday.	13|Tuesday.	23|Friday.
3|Saturday.	14|Wednesday.	24|Saturday.
4|3 S. in Lent.	15|Thursday.	25|Palm Sun.
5|Monday.	16|Friday.	26|Monday.
6|Tuesday.	17|Saturday.	27|Tuesday.
7|Wednesday.	18|5 S in Lent.	28|Wednesday.
8|Thursday.	19|Monday.	29|Thursday.—
9|Friday.	20|Tuesday.	30|Good Friday.
10|Saturday.	21|Wednesday.	31|Saturday.
11|4 S. in Lent.		

For lo, the winter is past, the rain is over and gone;

The flowers appear on the earth; the time of the singing of birds is come, and the voice of the turtle-dove is heard in our land.

Song of Solomon 2:11–12

Elizabeth Barrett Browning born, 1806.

Young men, ay and maids,
Too often sow their wild oats in tame verse.

EBB

Great Britain's Royal Horticultural Society is founded by John Wedgwood, Josiah's son, 1804.

Molly Mogg dies in 1766; immortalized in poems by Gay, Pope, and Swift, mistakenly attributing to her the beauty of her sister Suzy.

In 1858, woman is rescued after forty-three hours in a snowbank; she lives to tell the tale.

The first woman obtains a pilot's license; in Paris, Baroness Raymonde de Laroche, 1910.

Marriage of Napoleon and Josephine, 1796.

Bombe Josephine: Chill a 1-quart bombe mold in the freezer. Line inside of mold with ½ pint softened coffee ice-cream, return mold to freezer. When lining is hard, fill center with 1 pint pistachio ice-cream; let this harden and fill the rest of the mold with ½ pint coffee ice cream. Unmold when frozen.

After having been engaged to seven other princesses, Charles V of Spain marries Isabella of Portugal. 1526.

March.

1 2 SUN. IN LENT.
2 Monday.
3 Tuesday.
4 Wednesday.
5 Thursday.
6 Friday.
7 Saturday.
8 3 SUN. IN LENT.
9 Monday.
10 Tuesday.
11 Wednesday.
12 Thursday.
13 Friday.
14 Saturday.
15 4 SUN. IN LENT.
16 Monday.
17 Tuesday.
18 Wednesday.
19 Thursday.
20 Friday.
21 Saturday.
22 5 SUN. IN LENT.
23 Monday.
24 Tuesday.
25 W. Lady Day.
26 Thursday.
27 Friday.
28 Saturday.
29 PALM SUNDAY.
30 Monday.
31 Tuesday.

Last Quarter.
8th day, 6 h. 54 m. aftern.
New Moon.
16th day, 5 h. 37 m. aftern.
First Quarter.
23rd day, 5 h. 23 m. aftern.
Full Moon.
30th day, 4 h. 40 m. aftern.

Shad is a fish native to American waters; the Dutch settlers called it *elft*, which means "eleventh", because the first day for catching shad was March 11th. It was one of George Washington's favorite dishes.

To clean raw silks and ribbons, an old housekeeping book recommends paring four or five good-sized potatoes, slicing them very thin, and laying them in a quart of cold water for a few hours. The silk should be sponged with the potato water and ironed dry; the starch from the potatoes is said to cleanse the silk and give it a little stiffness.

An old superstition says that it is best to sow and transplant when the moon is waxing, never when it is waning. This has recently been proven true scientifically.

13

Planet Uranus discovered, 1781.

❧

I wandered lonely as a cloud
That floats on high o'er vales and hills,
When all at once I saw a crowd,
A host, of golden daffodils;
Beside the lake, beneath the trees,
Fluttering and dancing in the breeze.

Wordsworth

14

Johann Strauss born, 1804.

In ancient Rome, the festival of the "Old Mars". Men clad in skins led an old man called *Mamurius Veturius* —Old Mars—through the streets, beating him with sticks and driving him out of town. The old man represented the out-worn deity of vegetation, who had to be replaced by a fresh and vigorous new god at the beginning of a new year.

15

(The Ides of March)
The assassination of Julius Caesar in 44 B.C.

❧

In 1830 Murdoch Grant, an itinerant peddler, is murdered. The criminal was detected with the help of a voice in a dream, which spoke in Gaelic and gave a local citizen details of the crime.

SIMNEL CAKE

16

In Britain, the fourth Sunday in Lent is known as Mothering Sunday, or Midlent. It was the custom in earlier days for young people who had gone into service or apprenticeships to call on their mothers on that day bringing gifts—a bouquet of violets or a rich fruit cake called Simnel-cake.

To avoid clothes freezing on the line, mix one pint of salt with one pint of hot water, and rub this on the line where the clothes are hung.

Hair clippings—from people or pets—put into the holes where beans are planted provide trace minerals to nourish the soil.

Crumbled mothballs mixed with the soil where carrots are planted will discourage the larvae of the carrot fly.

Richard Burbage, actor in Shakespeare's company, dies in 1619. His tombstone reads EXIT BURBAGE.

A violet in the youth of primy nature,
Forward, not permanent, sweet, not lasting.
The perfume and suppliance of a minute.
Shakespeare, Hamlet

17

Noah is said to have gone into the Ark on this day.

GLOBE THEATRE

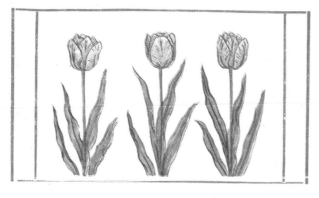

Kate Greenaway born, 1846.

The day of St. Patrick, patron saint of Ireland.
Among his less well-known miracles is the following:

> Saint Patrick, as in legends told,
> The morning being very cold,
> In order to assuage the weather,
> Collected bits of ice together;
> Then gently breathed upon the pyre,
> When every fragment blazed on fire.

St. Gertrude's Day. She was regarded a help against plagues of mice and rats.

In the region of Freising, Germany, there was a plague of mice in 1233 so terrible that whole towns were abandoned by populations fleeing the pests.

18

The first public buses in Europe were run in Paris in 1662, under Louis XIV. Intended for the city's poor, who could not afford to hire carriages, the buses became a fad among the fashionable, who jammed them for the first months. After that, the poor would have nothing to do with them and the service was discontinued.

Paper kites were introduced in Europe at the end of the 1600s by travellers returning from China.

19

This is the day the swallows return to the San Juan Capistrano Mission in California. According to tradition (though not to biologists), the swallows return on exactly this date every year, even in leap years.

20

Henrik Ibsen born, 1828.

What's a man's first duty? The answer's brief: to be himself.
H. Ibsen

SPRING.

SPRING, THE SWEET SPRING

Spring, the sweet spring, is the year's pleasant king
Then blooms each thing, then maids dance in a ring,
Cold doth not sing, the pretty birds do sing:
Cuckoo, jug-jug, pu-we, to-witaa-woo!

Thomas Nash

MARCH.

1. Thursday.	17. Saturday.
2. Friday.	18. SUNDAY.
3. Saturday.	19. Monday.
4. SUNDAY.	20. Tuesday.
5. Monday.	21. Wednesday.
6. Tuesday.	22. Thursday.
7. Wednesday.	23. GOOD FRIDAY
8. Thursday.	24. Saturday.
9. Friday.	25. EASTER SUNDAY.
10. Saturday.	26. Monday.
11. SUNDAY.	27. Tuesday.
12. Monday.	28. Wednesday.
13. Tuesday.	29. Thursday.
14. Wednesday.	30. Friday.
15. Thursday.	31. Saturday.
16. Friday.	

21

ARIES   ♈   The Ram.

The sun enters the first zodiac sign of the year, Aries.

The day of the vernal equinox, the first day of spring, when the day and the night are of equal length.

When swamps thaw out in March and the warmth lasts on into the evening, one of the first sounds of spring in North America is the voice of the tiny frog known as the spring peeper.

Johann Sebastian Bach born, 1685.

One of the first green things to be seen in March is the skunk cabbage coming up in swamps and woods. Skunk cabbage comes from a family of tropical plants, and mysteriously produces its own heat. The plant's temperature can be as much as 27°F higher than the temperature of its surroundings, so its shoots can melt their way through the frozen earth.

22

SPRING

Nothing is so beautiful as spring—
    When weeds, in wheels, shoot long and lovely and lush;
    Thrush's eggs look like low heavens, and thrush
Through the echoing timber does so rinse and wring
The ear, it strikes like lightning to hear him sing;
    The glassy peartree leaves and blooms, they brush
    The descending blue; that blue is all in a rush
With richness; the racing lambs too have fair their fling.
Gerard Manley Hopkins

In the spring a young man's fancy lightly turns
to thoughts of love.
Tennyson

The earliest possible Easter. It happened in 1818 and will not occur again until 2285.

In March is good grafting, the skillful do know
so long as the wind in the East do not blow.

Death of Goethe in 1832, aged 83 and hailed as one of Germany's greatest men. His last words were "More light!"

Old books on farming generally tell the farmer to "look to his fences" in March. The March wind dries out wood stored over the winter, and this is the time for splitting rails.

 23

The sugar maple tree is native to North America. The Indians of the Northeast introduced maple sugar to the white settlers. March is the time for tapping maple trees: The sap rises when freezing nights alternate with warm days, and there is still snow on the ground. The Indians used maple sugar as Europeans used salt, to flavor everything.

Maple Beer—To 4 gallons of boiling water add 1 quart of maple syrup, and a small tablespoon of essence of spruce. When it is about milk-warm, add 1 pint of yeast; and when fermented, bottle it. In 3 days it is fit to use.

Playing cards are first mentioned in writing, Florence, 1377.

24

Queen Elizabeth I dies on this day in the year 1603, aged 70.

25

Annunciation Day. Celebrates the Angel Gabriel's announcement to Mary that she would be the mother of Jesus. It is called Waffle Day in Sweden and waffles are eaten on this day.

26

If it thunders in March one may well say "alas" *(helas)*.
French proverb

The unpredictable changes of temperature in March often cause colds. A nineteenth century remedy for sore throats was to put a red stocking around your neck before going to bed.

Wine whey for restoring strength: Mix 1 pint of milk with 2 glasses of wine. Let it stand for 12 minutes, strain through a muslin bag, sweeten with loaf sugar.

A tea made from 1 ounce of dried elder flowers, 1 ounce of dried peppermint leaves, and 1½ pints of boiling water is said to help reduce the fever in colds. The boiling water should be poured over the herbs, and the tea left to steep covered for 15 minutes.

27

In Bavarian folk belief, one who eats blutwurst before sunrise will have money and good health all year; he who eats it sober will never suffer from flea bites and rashes.

28

The first washing machine is patented in the U.S., 1797.

When the weather starts to get mild, children like to go outside and play tag, a very old running-and-catching game. The child who is "it" can tag another unless the other player is touching something made of wood. In earlier times, and up until today in some parts of America, the other player had to be touching something made of *iron* to be safe. In folktales, fairies and goblins are afraid of iron—so this game goes back to the idea of being chased by a demon.

29

To get rid of the barnyard smell of new feathers for stuffing pillows, ask the baker to put them in his oven for one or two nights.

March borrows of April
Three days, and they be ill;
April borrows of March again
Three days of wind and rain.

March.

1	3 S. IN LENT	17	ST. PATRICK
2	Monday	18	Wednesday
3	Tuesday	19	Thursday
4	Wednesday	20	Friday
5	Thursday	21	Saturday
6	Friday	22	PALM SUN.
7	Saturday	23	Monday
8	4 S. IN LENT	24	Tuesday
9	Monday	25	LADY DAY
10	Tuesday	26	Thursday
11	Wednesday	27	GOOD FRI.
12	Thursday	28	Saturday
13	Friday	29	EASTER S.
14	Saturday	30	BANK HOL.
15	5 S. IN LENT	31	Tuesday
16	Monday		

daffodils,
Which come before the swallow dares, and take
The winds of March with beauty.

Shakespeare, The Winter's Tale

30

PALM SUNDAY

31

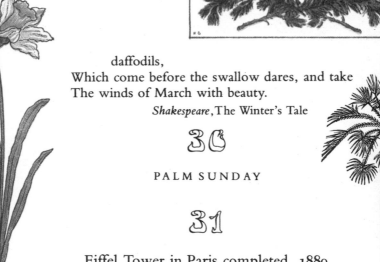

Eiffel Tower in Paris completed, 1889.

Death of Francis I in 1547, brought on "by immorality". At his funeral, the sermon suggested he had gone straight to heaven without passing through purgatory; the bishop was rebuked and the sermon was never published.

AVRIL

APRIL

April.

1	Tuesday	16	Wednesday
2	Wednesday	17	Thursday
3	Thursday	18	Friday
4	*Good Friday*	19	Saturday
5	Saturday	20	2 S. AF. EAS.
6	EASTER S.	21	Monday
7	Bank Holid.	22	Tuesday
8	Tuesday	23	Wednesday
9	Wednesday	24	Thursday
10	Thursday	25	Friday
11	Friday	26	Saturday
12	Saturday	27	3 S. AF. EAS.
13	Low SUN.	28	Monday
14	Monday	29	Tuesday
15	Tuesday	30	Wednesday

Proud-pied April dressed in all his trim
Hath put a spirit of youth in everything.

Shakespeare

1

APRIL FOOL'S DAY

The origin of April Fool's Day is not clear; it has been traced only to the 18th century in England and the 16th century in France. Remarkably, the Hindus have a similar festival, the Huli, at about this time, which includes prankishly sending off people with messages to nonexistent or absent persons.

✑

The 16th century calendar change made the year begin on January 1 instead of March 25 in parts of Europe. Pranksters continued making New Year's calls at the end of March.

✑

In most places, the rule is that April Fool-ing is to end at noon, and anyone who tries to play a joke later in the day is the fool.

The Duke of Lorraine and his wife escape from Nantes prison because they attempt it on April Fool's Day. As they were leaving the city disguised as peasants, a woman recognized them and hurried to inform the guard. The soldier, however, suspecting an April Fool's joke, cried April Fool! and did nothing.

First mention of the hackney-coach stand, ancestor of the taxi stand, 1634. A coachowner stationed four of his vehicles at a street corner in London, and a dozen other drivers followed suit. Pamphlets were published attacking the coaches. It was claimed that the noise they made shook casements, soured beer, ale, and wine, and interfered with the practice of religion by drowning out the preacher's sermon.

2

Hans Christian Andersen born, 1805.

First motion-picture theatre in the United States opens, in a shop in Los Angeles, 1902.

The surgeon Leon Labbé presents to the French Académie des Sciences a fork he has removed from the stomach of a Paris department-store worker (who is from then on called the Forkman [*L'homme a la fourchette*]). This was the first such operation. Paris, 1876.

3

MAUNDY MONEY

The day before Good Friday, called Maundy Thursday, marked by acts of humility and charity. By custom the old British monarchs had brought before them as many poor men as they were years old. The King or Queen would wash the feet of their subjects and give them baskets—"maunds"—of food.

Washington Irving born, 1783.

The Pony Express starts service, 1860; couriers set off on this day from St. Joseph, Missouri, and San Francisco. The 1,900-mile (3057 km) trip is made in about ten days—an average of eight miles per hour.

4

GOOD FRIDAY

On Good Friday at St. Bartholomew the Great , a church in London, wardens placed twenty-one new sixpences on the tomb of a former benefactor of the church. The coins were picked up by twenty-one widows, each of whom received a hot cross bun and then walked across the tombstone.

April.

1	Easter S.	11	Wednesday.	21	Saturday.
2	Bank Holid.	12	Thursday.	22	3 S. Aft. Eas.
3	Tuesday.	13	Friday.	23	Monday.
4	Wednesday.	14	Saturday.	24	Tuesday.
5	Thursday.	15	2 S. Aft. Eas	25	Wednesday.
6	Friday.	16	Monday.	26	Thursday.
7	Saturday.	17	Tuesday.	27	Friday.
8	Low Sun.	18	Wednesday.	28	Saturday.
9	Monday.	19	Thursday.	29	4 S. Aft. Eas.
10	Tuesday.	20	Friday.	30	Monday.

Hot cross buns!
Hot cross buns!
One a penny, two a penny,
Hot cross buns!
If your daughters do not like them
Give them to your sons;
But if you haven't any of these pretty little elves
You cannot do better than eat them yourselves.

5

19th century babies wore amber beads to avert croup.

6

EASTER SUNDAY

The egg is a symbol of rebirth at springtime. Gifts of eggs and games involving eggs are universal customs at Easter.

In pre-Christian times, Romans held running races at this time of year on egg-shaped tracks and gave eggs as prizes.

On Easter Day all the young people come out in something new and bright like butterflies. It is almost part of their religion to wear something new on this day. It was an old saying that if you don't wear something new on Easter Day, the crows will spoil everything you have on.

Francis Kilvert

He who is born on Easter morn
Will never know want or care or harm.

First Olympic Games in modern times are held in 1896 in Greece.

7

EASTER MONDAY

William Wordsworth born, 1770.

In an old English town, Hallaton, Easter Monday was Hare Pie Scrambling and Bottle Kicking Day. These events took place on a nearby green after church services.

In parts of Britain until very recently a strange custom called "heaving" was practiced on the Monday and Tuesday following Easter Sunday. On the first day, women would capture men and heave them up in the air; the next day the roles would be reversed. This is said to represent the Resurrection, but is probably left over from a pagan rite to promote the growth of crops.

Buddha's birthday is celebrated around this time in Hawaii, Japan, and Korea. In Japan, his statue is bathed with hydrangea-leaf tea.

9

Charles Baudelaire born, 1821.

The first public art exhibition opens at the Palais-Royale in Paris, 1667.

10

Safety pin is patented, 1849. The patent was sold later for $400.

11

The premiere of George Bernard Shaw's play *Pygmalion*, 1914.

12

Until the last century, jump-rope was a town boys' activity. Jump-rope games with rhymes and displays of skill, as played by girls now, are quite new.

13

It is suggested that April derives from the Latin term *aperio*—"I open". It has also been conjectured that the origin of the word was Aphrodite (Aphrilis, Aprilis, April?) because the month was associated with the reproductive powers of nature. Saxons called it *Oster monath*, perhaps for its prevalent east winds.

14

All unlicensed mountebanks are outlawed. The Master of Revels was allowed by the King to tax all funmakers, 1684.

15

PASSOVER

Passover celebrates the Jews' deliverance from Egypt, but it is also a spring festival. It is observed for seven days in Israel, eight elsewhere. Because the Jewish calendar is based on the phases of the moon, it is assumed that Jews living away from Israel might not be sure when the holiday actually starts, so they take an extra day to be certain.

❧

Leonardo da Vinci born, 1452.

16

Charlie Chaplin born, 1889.

❧

Well-apparell'd April on the heel of limping winter treads.

Shakespeare, Romeo & Juliet

17

In 1725 John Rudge bequeaths to his church twenty shillings a year to pay a man charged with keeping people awake and evicting dogs during services.

Many nobles of Europe have been known for their love of dogs, and they have often had their portraits painted with their favorite pets at their sides. Without doubt, the greatest dog lover of them all was Prince Karl Theodor of Bavaria, who kept 800 of all kinds.

18

The first train in Asia, 1853. Great Indian Peninsula Railway, Bombay to Tanna, 22 miles (36 km).

19

Queen Christina, who abdicated the Swedish throne in order to gratify her intellectual yearnings, dies this day in 1689.

20

In 1841 the first detective story was published—Edgar Allan Poe's *Murders in the Rue Morgue.*

In ancient Egypt, all-night parties were held to celebrate ten-day-old babies.

Spring hangs her infant blossoms on the trees,
Rock'd in the cradle of the western breeze.
William Cowper

21

TAURUS   ♉   *The Bull.*

The sun enters the second zodiac sign of the year, Taurus.

The founding of Rome in 753 B.C.

In ancient Rome, during the festival of the Parilia, fires scented with laurel and rosemary were passed among the sheep and cattle to purify them. Shepherds and animals also lept through bonfires.

22

The first known roller skates are worn by a young Belgian musical-instrument maker in 1760. He rolls into a party in London playing the violin, but is unable to stop and crashes into a mirror.

In 1903 a German glasscutter built a working grandfather's clock which, with the exception of the spring, was made completely of glass.

23

William Shakespeare born, 1564.

O how this spring of love resembleth
  The uncertain glory of an April day,
Which now shows all the beauty of the sun,
  And by and by a cloud takes all away!

Shakespeare, Two Gentlemen of Verona

Founding of the Order of the Garter,
the oldest order of knighthood, in 1347.

April.

1	Wednesday	16	Thursday
2	Thursday	17	Friday
3	Friday	18	Saturday
4	Saturday	19	3 S. A. EAST.
5	Low Sun.	20	Monday
6	Monday	21	Tuesday
7	Tuesday	22	Wednesday
8	Wednesday	23	St. GEORGE
9	Thursday	24	Friday
10	Friday	25	Saturday
11	Saturday	26	4 S. A. EAST.
12	2 S. A. EAST.	27	Monday
13	Monday	28	Tuesday
14	Tuesday	29	Wednesday
15	Wednesday	30	Thursday

St. George's Day. St. George is noted
for slaying a dragon in Libya in the 3rd
century. He became the patron saint of
England because he appeared as an apparition in the sky during the Crusades,
frightening the Moslem enemies of the
Crusaders.

24

APRIL.

1. Sunday.	16. Monday.
2. Monday.	17. Tuesday.
3. Tuesday.	18. Wednesday.
4. Wednesday.	19. Thursday.
5. Thursday.	20. Friday.
6. Friday.	21. Saturday.
7. Saturday.	22. Sunday.
8. Sunday.	23. Monday.
9. Monday.	24. Tuesday.
10. Tuesday.	25. Wedne-day.
11. Wednesday.	26. Thursday.
12. Thursday.	27. Friday.
13. Friday.	28. Saturday.
14. Saturday.	29. Sunday.
15. Sunday.	30. Monday.

Marry in April when you can,
Joy for maiden and for man.

St. Mark's Eve. In northern England it is believed that if you keep watch over a graveyard on this night, you will see apparitions of all who will be buried there in the coming year. On the light-hearted side, girls would attempt to divine the identity of their future husbands. One custom was to lay a row of nuts on the embers of a fire, whispering the name of one's beloved. Popping was a good omen; silent consumption by the fire was not.

25

London: Publication of *Robinson Crusoe* by Daniel Defoe, 1719.

The latest possible Easter occurred in 1943. This will happen again in 2038.

26

Audubon born, 1785. He toured Europe to raise subscriptions for his volumes of bird studies in 1826; the names of the kings of France and England headed his list.

Houseplants can be given spring vacations outdoors, but they should not be exposed immediately to direct sunlight.

Peppercorn Day in Bermuda: A rent of one peppercorn is collected for the use of an old building in St. George.

27

The first raincoat was made by François Fresnau, an engineer in French Guiana who made an old overcoat waterproof by coating it with latex from rubber trees.

The first mention of umbrellas appeared in 1637, in a list of the belongings of Louis XIII. The list included: eleven sunshades in various colors made of taffeta; three umbrellas of oiled cloth trimmed underneath with gold and silver lace.

Until late in the 18th century, umbrellas were considered feminine, and men were ridiculed for carrying them. They were also expensive and were often rented out by coffeehouses or churches.

28

Mutiny on the *Bounty*, 1789.

Oh, to be in England
Now that April's there.
Robert Browning

April.

1	Wednesday.
2	Thursday.
3	*Good Friday.*
4	Saturday.
5	EASTER SUN.
6	Bank Holiday.
7	Tuesday.
8	Wednesday.
9	Thursday.
10	Friday.
11	Saturday.
12	LOW SUNDAY.
13	Monday.
14	Tuesday.
15	Wednesday.
16	Thursday.
17	Friday.
18	Saturday.
19	2 S. AFT. EAST.
20	Monday.
21	Tuesday.
22	Wednesday.
23	Thursday.
24	Friday.
25	Saturday.
26	3 S. AFT. EAST.
27	Monday.
28	Tuesday.
29	Wednesday.
30	Thursday.

Last Quarter.
7th day, 2 h. 43 m. aftern.
New Moon.
15th day, 5 h. 51 m. morn.
First Quarter.
21st day, 11 h. 20 m. aftern.
Full Moon.
29th day, 6 h. 14 m. morn.

April brings the primrose sweet,
Scatters daisies at our feet.
Sara Coleridge

In ancient Rome, the first day of the weeklong Festival of Flora.

Both eggs and seeds for planting can be tested by the same method: a good seed or a good egg sinks to the bottom of a pan of water. Those that float should be discarded.

29

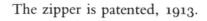

The zipper is patented, 1913.

When April blows his horn it's good for both hay and corn.

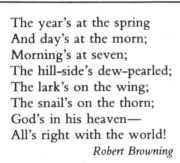

The year's at the spring
And day's at the morn;
Morning's at seven;
The hill-side's dew-pearled;
The lark's on the wing;
The snail's on the thorn;
God's in his heaven—
All's right with the world!

Robert Browning

The nightingale is preëminently the bird of April. They sing most strongly in this month, as they have not yet become distracted by the chores of rearing a family. Sir John Sinclair hoped to establish nightingales in his native Scotland. He purchased as many eggs as he could for a shilling apiece and had them mailed to Scotland, where his deputies placed them in preselected robins' nests. The birds hatched and, as fall approached, migrated. However, they did not return as Sir John had hoped, and were never seen again.

30

Walpurgis Night. Bonfires to ward off evil spirits were lit all over Germany and Scandinavia starting in pre-Christian times.

Sweete April showers,
Doo spring Maie flowers.

April, April,
Laugh thy girlish laughter;
Then, the moment after,
Weep thy girlish tears!
William Watson

The April's in her eyes: it is love's spring,
And these the showers to bring it on.
Shakespeare, Antony & Cleopatra

It was a lover and his lass
With a hey, and a ho, and a hey nonino
That o'er the freen corn-fields did pass
In the spring time, the only pretty ring time,
When birds do sing, hey ding a ding ding:
Sweet lovers love the spring.
Shakespeare, As You Like It

MAI

MAY

May.

1	Thursday	17	Saturday
2	Friday	18	S. af. Asc.
3	Saturday	19	Monday
4	4 S. af. Eas.	20	Tuesday
5	Monday	21	Wednesday
6	Tuesday	22	Thursday
7	Wednesday	23	Friday
8	Thursday	24	Saturday
9	Friday	25	Whit Sun.
10	Saturday	26	Bank Holid.
11	Rogatn. S.	27	Tuesday
12	Monday	28	Wednesday
13	Tuesday	29	Thursday
14	Wednesday	30	Friday
15	Ascen. Day	31	Saturday
16	Friday		

The word May is a perfumed word. It is an illuminated initial. It means youth, love, song, and all that is beautiful in life.

Longfellow, Journal

1

MAY DAY

May Day is traditionally the last of the series of rites celebrating the arrival of spring. In medieval England it was customary to "go a-Maying", fetching hawthorn blossoms and bedecking the houses. The prettiest girl was crowned Queen of May and a tall pole was set up and hung with flowers. Even royalty joined in these festivities. These charming celebrations of nature have not, unfortunately, survived the industrial age. The only May Day custom still widely observed is that practiced by young girls who wash their faces with the first dew of the morning to ensure a lovely complexion.

Maypole dances come from the old Roman Floralalia, a festival of flowers held in May.

In Sweden, a sham battle is held on May Day between boys representing Winter and Summer—Summer always wins.

But their chiefest jewel they bring from thence is their maypole, which they bring home with great veneration, as thus: They have twenty or forty yoke of oxen, every ox having a sweet nosegay of flowers tied on the tip of his horns, and these oxen draw home this maypole (this stinking idol rather), which is covered all over with flowers and herbs, bound about with strings, from the top to the bottom, and sometimes painted with variable colours, with two or three hundred men, women and children following it, with great devotion. And thus being reared up, with handkerchiefs and flags streaming at the top, they strew the ground about, bind green boughs about it, set up summer halls, bowers and arbours hard by it. And then they fall to banquet and feast, to leap and dance about it, as the heathen people did, at the dedication of their idols, whereof this is a perfect pattern, or rather the thing itself.

Philip Stubbes, 16th century Puritan

Yougthes folke now flocken in everywhere,
To gather may buskets and smelling brere:
And home they hasten the postes to dight
And all the Kirke pillours eare day light,
With hawthorn buds and swete eglantine,
And girlonds of roses, and sopps in wine.

Spenser

There was a May Day poetry competition in Provence, with flowers made of gold and silver awarded to the champions. The contest was financed by a bequest of a lady of rank in 1540 and the tradition survived until the Revolution.

❧

It is an old American May Day custom, which still exists in some places, for children to make paper baskets, fill them with candies and wildflowers, and hang them on the door of a special friend.

❧

May Day is Labor Day in many parts of Europe.

Ash and hickory wood for barrels and hoops are at their best if they are cut in May, when they contain their highest percentage of oil. Wood cut in May is good for making tool handles, too.

Machiavelli born, 1469.

MINT

The Kentucky Derby is run on the first Saturday in May. The mint julep, a Derby-time tradition, was originally a mint tea with a bit of whiskey in it. It was used as a cold remedy and, with a bit more whiskey, as a morning-after drink.

In 1810 Lord Byron swims the Hellespont, in Turkey, in one hour, ten minutes.

In May get a weede hooke, a crotch and a glove, and weed out such weedes as the corn doth not love.

Flowers before May bring bad luck.

Welsh proverb

Rough winds do shake the darling buds of May,

Shakespeare

A belief: The stroking of a basil plant, which scents the hand, is also helpful to the plant and keeps it alive.

St. Florian's Day. The patron saint of blacksmiths and firemen. This is a day to take fire-prevention measures.

Near North Bend, Ohio, in 1865, the first train robbery in the United States took place.

The ancients called all the sprouts of young vegetables "asparagus", but the name is reserved now for the vegetable that begins to be available in early spring.

May is the time to eat dandelion greens—later on they are tough.

From 1227 to 1589 it was customary for the youngest peer in France to present a tribute of roses to the French Parlement on this day. It supposedly commemorated the youthful noble who, reminded of his duty, tore himself away from lovemaking to prepare a case he was to plead before Parlement. The presentation of roses was supposed to show nobility's respect for the institution of Parlement.

Paris Exposition, 1900; opening day, 500,000 visitors.

Robert Browning born, 1812.

Beethoven, already deaf, conducts the first performance of his Ninth Symphony, in 1823, in Vienna.

By tradition, the day the storks return to Ribe, Denmark, where they nest on the roofs of houses.

Captain Barclay Allardice, famed pedestrian, died in 1854. He once walked 1,000 miles (1609 km) in 1,000 hours; wagers of 100,000 pounds rested on the outcome.

When the bridge at Niagara Falls was built, kites were used to carry cables across the river.

10

Wife as you will
now ply your still.

❦

Love, whose month is ever May,
Spied a blossom passing fair
Playing in the wanton air;
Shakespeare, Love's Labour's Lost

❦

Hard is his heart that loveth naught in May.
Chaucer

❦

Chaucer described Heaven as a place of
eternal "grene and lusty May".

❦

May.

1 Tuesday.	12 Saturday.	22 Tuesday.
2 Wednesday.	13 S. AFT. ASC.	23 Wednesday.
3 Thursday.	14 Monday.	24 Thursday.
4 Friday.	15 Tuesday.	25 Friday.
5 Saturday.	16 Wednesday.	26 Saturday.
6 ROGATION S.	17 Thursday.	27 TRINITY S.
7 Monday.	18 Friday.	28 Monday.
8 Tuesday.	19 Saturday.	29 Tuesday.
9 Wednesday.	20 WHIT SUN.	30 Wednesday.
10 Ascen. Day.	21 Bank Holid.	31 Thursday.
11 Friday.		

South German farmers sometimes like to feed cattle black bread
spread with early morning dew.

Cows in pasture thrive on fresh May grass. Saxons called May
Thrimilce because they could milk their cows three times each day
instead of twice.

11

Beginning today, the three-day festivals of the "Frost Saints" —Mammertus, Pancras, and Servatus. People in the wine-growing regions of France blame these saints for late frosts that damage the vines, and retaliate by defacing pictures of them.

The second Sunday in May is Mother's Day in the United States. It was proposed by Anna Jarvis of Philadelphia in 1907—no one in Congress dared vote against the idea.

12

The first official Mother's Day in the United States, 1914.

The first time a baby boy moved, in early American custom, he was carried upstairs with something silver or gold in his hand, to bring him wealth and cause him to rise in the world.

On Rogation days—the Monday, Tuesday, and Wednesday before Ascension Day, or Holy Thursday, it was the ancient custom in England to walk the boundaries of the parish. This had two objectives: (1) to ask divine blessings on the fruits of the earth, and (2) to preserve a correct knowledge of, and due respect for, the bounds of parochial and individual property. To assert these boundary rights, parishioners waded along rivers, swam canals, and walked through houses that were located on the boundary line. In America, families would walk the boundaries of their own land and "bump" the boys of the family against marker trees or boundary stones.

13

Sir Arthur Sullivan born, 1842.

❧

In Germany, one occasionally hears people speak of having "heartworm". An old Bavarian manuscript says that this is a worm "which bites at peoples' hearts"; it was supposed to have little horns like deers' antlers.

14

A swarm of bees in May
Is worth a load of hay.

❧

Take heede to thy bees that are readie to swarme,
the losse thereof now is a crownes worth of harme.

15

ASCENSION DAY

The fortieth day after Easter, a Thursday, is regarded as the day Jesus went to heaven. The weather is expected to be nice on this day because Jesus is said to have "kissed the clouds".

❧

Lyman Frank Baum, the author of the *Wizard of Oz* books, born, 1856.

❧

In England, people decorate their wells on Ascension Day with flowered trellises. The water is thanked and blessed.

❧

In ancient Rome, the festival of the Fontanalia was held at this time, to honor the spirits of springs, streams, and fountains.

16

Day of St. Brendan, the 6th-century Irishman who sailed west in search of the Garden of Eden. The fanciful account of his seven-year voyage, during which he is believed by some to have reached America, was said to have inspired Columbus. Patent grants on St. Brendan's mythical island were granted as late as the 17th century.

17

In the middle ages, manuscript books were so precious that one abbot gave an entire vineyard in exchange for a single missal.

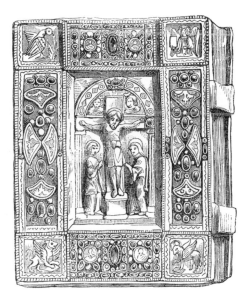

MAY.

1. Tuesday.	16. Wednesday.
2. Wednesday.	17. Thursday.
3. Thursday.	18. Friday.
4. Friday.	19. Saturday.
5. Saturday.	20. TRINITY SUNDAY.
6. SUNDAY.	21. Monday.
7. Monday.	22. Tuesday.
8. Tuesday.	23. Wednesday.
9. Wednesday.	24. Thursday.
10. Thursday.	25. Friday.
11. Friday.	26. Saturday.
12. Saturday.	27. SUNDAY.
13. WHIT SUNDAY.	28. Monday.
14. Monday.	29. Tuesday.
15. Tuesday.	30. Wednesday.
	31. Thursday.

18

Before the 19th century, many Germans refused to eat potatoes. American-born Count Rumford (Benjamin Thompson) introduced a Rumford soup—made mostly of potatoes—which reversed this resistance to the extent that potatoes became a favorite in Bavaria.

Early New Englanders believed that eating potatoes could shorten your life.

Mounts for the U.S. Army's camel corps arrive at the corps' base in Texas, 1856.

19

Napoleon establishes the Légion d'Honneur, 1802.

20

An ancient tradition at High Wycombe, Buckinghamshire, which has no explanation, was the public weighing on this day of the Mayor, Mayoress, Recorder, Town Clerk, and Alderman. Their weights were announced, and so was the difference between their weights that year and last.

May.

1 Friday.
2 Saturday.
3 4 S. AFT. EAST.
4 Monday.
5 Tuesday.
6 Wednesday.
7 Thursday.
8 Friday.
9 Saturday.
10 ROGATN. SUN.
11 Monday.
12 Tuesday.
13 Wednesday.
14 *Ascension Day.*
15 Friday.
16 Saturday.
17 S. AFT. ASCEN.
18 Monday.
19 Tuesday.
20 Wednesday.
21 Thursday.
22 Friday.
23 Saturday.
24 WHIT SUNDAY.
25 Bank Holiday.
26 Tuesday.
27 Wednesday.
28 Thursday.
29 Friday.
30 Saturday.
31 TRINITY SUN.

Last Quarter.
7th day, 8 h. 43 m. morn.
New Moon.
14th day, 3 h. 18 m. aftern.
First Quarter.
21st day, 5 h. 45 m. morn.
Full Moon.
28th day, 8 h. 31 m. aftern.

Eliza Donnithorne, believed to be the original of Miss Havisham in Dickens' *Great Expectations,* dies in Sidney, Australia, 1886. Jilted at the altar, she stopped the clocks in her large house and lived there in seclusion for the rest of her life—wearing her wedding gown and leaving her wedding cake untouched on the table every day for thirty years.

Place pieces of camphor, cedar-wood, Russia leather, tobacco-leaves, bog-myrtle, or anything else strongly aromatic, in the drawers or boxes where furs or other things to be preserved from moths are kept, and they will never take harm.

21

 . . . boys, intent upon their sport,
With twisted lash drive round some empty court
The whirling top.   *Virgil,* Aeneid

22

Sir Arthur Conan Doyle born, 1859.

In the 14th century, under Bavarian law, women were given the right to duel men to settle disputes.

23

Carolus Linnaeus, Swedish scientist known for his system of plant classification, born, 1707.

24

GEMINI   Ⅱ   *The Twins.*

The sun enters the third zodiac sign of the year, Gemini.

Birth of Queen Victoria, 1819; celebrated as Empire Day.

In 1844 Samuel F. B. Morse inaugurates the first telegraph line in America with the message "What hath God wrought!" transmitted between Washington, D.C., and Baltimore.

25

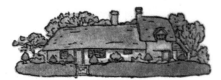

Flitting-day in Scotland, when the Scots move if they desire to change residence. On Candlemas Day (February 2), landlords are usually informed whether their tenants plan to "sit or flit".

PENTECOST

Pentecost is also called Whit Sunday, or Whitsunday, in England. It falls on the seventh Sunday after Easter and commemorates the miracle that began establishment of the Christian church: Suddenly, the apostles were able to speak all the languages they needed to spread the Christian message throughout the world.

At Haarlem, Holland, there is a flower festival that begins with a dramatic midnight display: Flower-sellers arrange their wares in the town square in the dark; at midnight, church bells peal, lights go on, and the festival begins.

May.

1	Friday	17	WHIT SUN.
2	Saturday	18	BANK HOL.
3	ROGATN. S.	19	Tuesday
4	Monday	20	Wednesday
5	Tuesday	21	Thursday
6	Wednesday	22	Friday
7	ASCEN. DAY	23	Saturday
8	Friday	24	TRINITY S.
9	Saturday	25	Monday
10	S. A. ASCEN.	26	Tuesday
11	Monday	27	Wednesday
12	Tuesday	28	CORP.CHRIS.
13	Wednesday	29	Friday
14	Thursday	30	Saturday
15	Friday	31	1 S. A. TRIN.
16	Saturday		

Whitsuntide was the favorite time of year for the Morris dance, which probably originated among the Moors (hence the name), then became connected with an ancient pageant celebrating Robin Hood. In 1599, William Kemp, a famous comic actor, Morris-danced from London to Norwich, a distance of 111 miles.

26

BRITISH SPRING HOLIDAY

Whit Monday was once celebrated on the day after Whit Sunday, and many old customs were related to the occasion.

According to a bequest made in 1675 in the English village of St. Ives, Huntingdonshire, children rolled dice for Bibles on Whit Monday. Until 1880 the dice rolling was done on the church altar.

At the Greenwich Fair, a feature of Whit Monday in the 18th century, a wild parade along Kent Road ended at the park with kiss-in-the-ring and a rough-and-tumble race down a slope. The fair was eventually prohibited because of the licentious character of the dancing.

At Dunmow, Essex, the Flitch of Bacon Trial has been held on this day since the 13th century. To earn the flitch of bacon, a couple must convince a jury of six maidens and six bachelors that they have been married for one year and one day without quarreling. The first winners were a sea-captain and his wife who hadn't seen each other since their wedding day. In 1841 the prize was offered to Victoria and Albert, who graciously declined it.

This trial was mentioned by Chaucer's Wife of Bath:

> Never for them the flitch of bacon though
> That some have won in Essex at Dunmow.

Whit Monday was moved to the last Monday in May in Britain, but that has become Spring Holiday and Whit Monday is all but forgotten.

27

Isadora Duncan born, 1878.

28

The Afsluitdijk, the longest sea dam in the world, is completed in 1932. It stretches over 20 miles (32.5 km) across the mouth of the Zuider Zee, creating a freshwater sea, the Ijsselmeer. The dam has a sea-level width of 293 feet (89 m) and is 24 feet 7 in. (7.5 m) high.

A Munich ordinance prohibited the wearing of caps pulled down over the face since, as it noted, "robbers, burglers, and poachers usually wear such hats to hide their faces". 1650.

29

In England, this is known as Royal Oak Day or Oak Apple Day. If schoolboys don't wear an oak leaf in their buttonholes or hats, other boys can flog them with nettles. This goes back to the restoration of Charles II to the British throne; he successfully hid from his enemies in an oak tree after the Battle of Worcester in 1651.

30

MEMORIAL DAY

First Memorial Day in the United States, 1868.

Day of St. Joan of Arc, patron saint of France.

31

Walt Whitman born, 1819.

An exhibit in 18th century Salem, Massachusetts: A "Sapient Dog" who could light lamps, spell, read print, tell time, and discharge a loaded canon. Admission, 25¢.

JUIN

JUNE

June.

1	TRINITY S.	11	Wednesday	21	Saturday
2	Monday	12	Thursday	22	3 S. AF. TRI.
3	Tuesday	13	Friday	23	Monday
4	Wednesday	14	Saturday	24	Tuesday
5	Thursday	15	2 S. AF. TRI.	25	Wednesday
6	Friday	16	Monday	26	Thursday
7	Saturday	17	Tuesday	27	Friday
8	1 S. AF. TRI.	18	Wednesday	28	Saturday
9	Monday	19	Thursday	29	4 S. AF. TRI.
10	Tuesday	20	*Queen's Accs.*	30	Monday

And what is so rare as a day in June?
Then, if ever, come perfect days.

James Russell Lowell

1

Ovid claims June was named after Juno, the goddess of love and marriage, but the month was apparently named after the Juniores, the minor house of the Roman legislature.

2

Day of St. Erasmus, patron saint of sailors; also known as St. Elmo's Day.

The premiere of *Les Sylphides*, with the first performance in Paris by Pavlova, 1909.

3

Skipping, jumping, and swinging are ancient devices used to make crops grow high. Skipping, as a child's game, prevails in spring months, when the shoots are coming up. In many places, swinging on a swing is a part of the ritual to encourage the growth of crops. Ancient Roman farmers hung balls, masks, and small images of the human figure, called *oscilla*, on trees or in doorways to swing in the wind.

Virgil wrote about farmers:
  They hail thee, Bacchus, in their merry lines,
  And hang their swinging puppets in the pines.

4

The custom in Europe is to plant a tree upon the birth of a baby: an apple tree for a boy, a pear tree for a girl.

5

In June 1647, many people saw a vision in the sky over New Haven, Connecticut, that revealed the tragic end of a ship that had not been heard from for six months. The ship was easily recognized by the townspeople, who watched its destruction in the apparition.

6

In Sitges, on the east coast of Spain, carnations grow wild. For the annual carnation show in early June, thousands of flowers are gathered to make a decorative carpet about a quarter-mile (400 m) long. A Catalan folk dance on the carpet pounds the flowers into perfume at the end of the day.

The first public museum, the Ashmolean, opens in Oxford, England, in 1683. Stuffed animals on exhibit include a dodo bird, and patrons are charged according to how long they stay in the museum.

7

A great battle between two swarms of bees in Cumberland, 1827. Some bee beliefs: Bees will not thrive if you quarrel over them. An unclaimed swarm settling on your property is bad luck. Bees should be informed when a death occurs and be invited to the funeral; crepe should be hung on the hive.

8

Strawberries can be preserved nicely in wine: Fill a pint jar with strawberries, add four tablespoons of sugar and Madeira wine.

9

The first Horn & Hardart Automat opens, in Philadelphia, 1902.

10

Time–observance Day in Japan, when people are supposed to be especially conscious of the importance of being punctual.

A swarm of bees in June
is worth a silver spoon.

11

To Preserve Cut Flowers

A bouquet of freshly-cut flowers may be preserved alive for a long time by placing them in a glass or vase with fresh water, in which a little charcoal has been steeped, or a small piece of camphor dissolved. The vase should be set upon a plate or dish, and covered with a bell-glass, around the edges of which, when it comes in contact with the plate, a little water should be poured to exclude the air.

 A pinch of salt in the vase can make flowers last longer.

12

To Make Conserve of Red Roses, or Any Other Flowers

Take rose buds or any other flowers and pick them, cut off the white part from the red, and put the red flowers in a sieve and sift them through to take out the seeds; then weigh them, and to every pound of flowers take two pounds and a half of loaf sugar; beat the flowers pretty fine in a stone mortar, then by degrees put the sugar to them, and beat it very well till it is well incorporated together; then put it into gallipots, tie it over with paper, over that a leather, and it will keep seven years.

Baseball invented by Abner Doubleday, in 1839.

13

JUNE.

1. Friday.	16. Saturday.
2. Saturday.	17. SUNDAY.
3. SUNDAY.	18. Monday.
4. Monday.	19. Tuesday.
5. Tuesday.	20. Wednesday.
6. Wednesday.	21. Thursday.
7. Thursday.	22. Friday.
8. Friday.	23. Saturday.
9. Saturday.	24 SUNDAY.
10. SUNDAY.	25. Monday.
11. Monday.	26. Tuesday.
12. Tuesday.	27. Wednesday.
13. Wednesday.	28. Thursday.
14. Thursday.	29. Friday.
15. Friday.	30. Saturday.

To Revive Cut Flowers After Packing

Plunge the stems into boiling water, and by the time the water is cold, the flowers will have revived. Then cut afresh the ends of the stems, and keep them in fresh cold water.

14

In 1777, the Continental Congress adopts the American flag.

Herbs for drying should be picked just after the dew dries, tied loosely, and hung in a high place.

If you want to dry herbs, now is the time to do it, before they bear blossoms.

Until well into the 19th century, Bavarian children were "struck out" of their grade at the end of the school year. They had to creep through the legs of the teacher and take a more-or-less light blow on the behind on the way. Then they paid a so-called "striking-out penny".

15

The rising of the Nile, originally believed to have its source in Paradise, usually takes place on this day. If it was late, a beautiful young girl was thrown in the waters to appease the gods. To Egyptians, Nile water once was to ordinary water what champagne is to wine; sacred bulls were not given it lest they grow too fat. When the Pasha of Egypt visited England in the 19th century, he brought his personal supply of Nile water for drinking.

Benjamin Franklin flies a kite in a storm in 1752 to prove that lightning is attracted to metal.

16

The first stone is laid in Schiedam, Holland, in 1794 for De Walvisch (The Whale), the biggest grain windmill in the world. It still exists.

To clean papered walls: The very best method is to rub with stale bread. Cut the crust off very thick, and wipe straight down from the top, then go to the top again, and so on. The staler the bread the better.

17

Postage stamps are introduced in Belgium, 1849.

An old Danish custom required the actual tying of a knot at a wedding, with two pieces of string or ribbon. This tradition spread to England and other parts of Europe and is the origin of the expression "to tie the knot".

18

In the Australian bush, weddings used to be occasions for "tin kettling", young men would make a racket with kerosene tins and fencing wire until the bride and groom invited them in for supper.

Old American wedding customs included the shivaree, a mock serenade with a raucous racket of pots and pans, cowbells, and shotgun fire outside the newlyweds' window.

The Romans considered June the most auspicious month for weddings, especially at a full moon or at conjuction of the sun and moon.

The custom of giving guests pieces of wedding cake to take home comes from an ancient Roman practice of breaking a cake over the bride's head for luck. People picked up the pieces for their own good luck.

If a medieval bridal party came across a monk, priest, hare, dog, cat, lizard, or serpent on the way to church, it was an inauspicious sign for the marriage.

19

June.

1 Friday.	11 Monday.	21 Thursday.
2 Saturday.	12 Tuesday.	22 Friday.
3 1 S AF.TRIN	13 Wednesday.	23 Saturday.
4 Monday.	14 Thursday.	24 4 S.AF.TRIN
5 Tuesday.	15 Friday.	25 Monday.
6 Wednesday	16 Saturday.	26 Tuesday.
7 Thursday.	17 3 S.AF.TRIN.	27 Wednesday.
8 Friday.	18 Monday.	28 Thursday.
9 Saturday.	19 Tuesday.	29 Friday.
10 2 S.AF.TRIN.	20 Queen'sAccs	30 Saturday.

Marry when June roses grow,
Over land and sea you'll go.

Shift marriages, a widely practiced early American custom: A widowed woman whose new husband did not want to assume debts left by her previous husband would be married wearing only her shift. The ceremony usually took place at night on a crossroads.

Harming a robin is extremely bad luck. If you take their eggs, your legs will break. If you are holding one when it dies, your hand will always shake.

Alexander L. Hamehameha IV, king of the Hawaiian Islands, marries Emma Rooke, the daughter of an English physician, in Honolulu, 1856.

20

A Command Performance by Buffalo Bill for Queen Victoria and her guests during her Golden Jubilee, in 1887. Four kings board the Deadwood coach, driven by Buffalo Bill.

SUMMER.

With the word the time will bring on summer,
When briers shall have leaves as well as thorns,
And be as sweet as sharp.

Shakespeare, All's Well That Ends Well

All the live murmur of a summer's day.

Matthew Arnold

21

Wedding rings go on the fourth finger because the ancients believed it contained a nerve going straight to the heart.

Sometimes a gimmal ring—three rings joined by a pivot—was used for weddings. At the ceremony the ring was broken up, with one going to each of the newlyweds and the third to the witness.

22

June 21–22 is the time of the summer solstice, the longest day.

The sun enters the fourth zodiac sign of the year, Cancer.

CANCER ♋ The Crab.

23

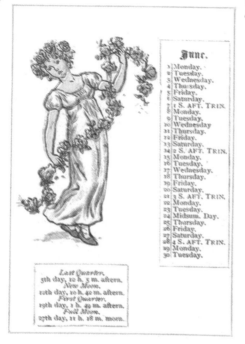

MIDSUMMER'S EVE

The biggest bonfire-lighting holiday of Europe is celebrated on the eve of the longest day in the year. The bonfires originally represented the sun. Midsummer's Eve bonfires are called St. John's Fires in honor of St. John's Day, which follows. The Irish believe that on Midsummer's Eve one's soul wanders from the body to the eventual place of death.

To Make Milk of Roses

Two ounces sweet almonds beaten to a paste, forty drops of oil of lavender, forty ounces of rose water.

24

MIDSUMMER'S DAY

Also St. John the Baptist's Day. There is an old belief that the sun spins in the sky on this day. In Cornwall, a Midsummer's Day bonfire is crowned with a witch's broom and hat and set on a hill to warn witches to stay away for a year. To break witches' spells, forty kinds of herbs are thrown into the fire.

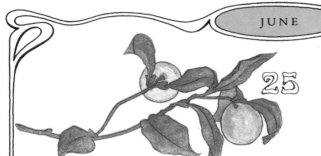

25

Orange blossoms have been worn at weddings for a very long time. The orange tree, which stays green all year, symbolizes eternal love.

It was a custom in the United States until at least 1783 for a group of young men, usually rejected suitors, to steal the bride after a wedding ceremony and return her to the groom only after a ransom of a supper for all had been paid.

In the Scottish custom of "creeling", a newly married man had to run with a basket of stones on his back until his wife caught up with him and gave him a kiss before the amused onlookers. The duration of the run depended upon the wife's physical condition, shyness, and sense of sport.

26

A Quicker Sort of Sweet Pot

Take three handfuls of orange-flowers, three of clove-gillyflowers, three of damask roses, one of knotted marjoram, one of lemon-thyme, six bay-leaves, a handful of rosemary, one of myrtle, half one of mint, one of lavender, the rind of a lemon, and a quarter of an ounce of cloves. Chop all; and put them in layers, with pounded bay-salt between, up to the top of the jar. If all the ingredients cannot be got at once, put them in as you get them; always throwing in salt with every new article.

27

The custom of carrying a bride over the threshold is probably left over from the days when men got their brides by capturing them. ❧

It was a medieval custom for friends to accompany the bridal pair when they bathed on their wedding night. A Regensburg ordinance of 1320 proclaimed that no more than 24 males and 8 females were permitted to attend on such occasions. ❧

Calm weather in June
Sets corn in tune.

NORWEGIAN BRIDE

June.

1	Monday	16	Tuesday
2	Tuesday	17	Wednesday
3	Wednesday	18	Thursday
4	Thursday	19	Friday
5	Friday	20	Ac. Qn. Vic.
6	Saturday	21	4 S. A. Trin.
7	2 S. A. Trin.	22	Monday
8	Monday	23	Tuesday
9	Tuesday	24	Midsum. D.
10	Wednesday	25	Thursday
11	Thursday	26	Friday
12	Friday	27	Saturday
13	Saturday	28	5 S. A. Trin.
14	3 S. A. Trin.	29	Monday
15	Monday	30	Tuesday

The cuckoo clock may have its origin in the medieval belief that the cuckoo—revered as the herald of spring—had supernatural powers that enabled it to tell how long one would live, in how many years one would marry, and so on, by uttering its call the appropriate number of times.

The ancients applied the term cuckoo to a wife's paramour; this referred to the cuckoo's habit of laying its eggs in other birds' nests to be hatched.

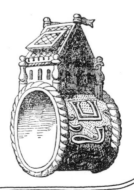

28

Bridesmaids are usually dressed alike. The ancient custom required the bride and several attendants to dress alike to confuse the evil spirits which had come to spoil the wedding.

The term "best man" is derived from old Scandinavian marriage customs. It was considered beneath a warrior's dignity to court a lady, so he would kidnap a bride on her way to her wedding. To guard against this, the groom sent his "best man" as an escort.

A brides should not wear pearls at her wedding: Pearls symbolize tears.

29

Day of St. Peter, patron saint of fishermen. The fishing fleet at Gloucester, Massachusetts, where the fishermen are of Italian and Portuguese descent, is blessed on St. Peter's Day.

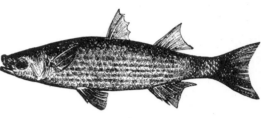

To celebrate the coronation of Queen Victoria, in 1838, the entire issue of the London newspaper *The Sun* is printed in gold ink.

To Wash White Lace

A quarter of a cake of white wax, six lumps of sugar, and a dessert-spoonful of made starch, to be mixed with a quart of soft water. Tuck the lace very slightly in a thin cloth, dipped in cold water, then let it lie in a strong lather for one day; change the water, and leave it in a second lather all night. Put the above materials into a saucepan, boil the lace in it for ten minutes, then throw it into cold water, and when nearly dry iron it.

30

Most early American remedies for baby ailments seem to be made with snails. One recipe calls for snails, earthworms, rosemary, bear's foot, agrimony, dock, barberries, wood sorrel, and rue.

A 971¾ carat diamond is found in 1893 in the Orange Freestate. The finder is rewarded with 500 pounds plus a horse with bridle and saddle.

July.

1	Tuesday	12	Saturday	23	Wednesday
2	Wednesday	13	6 S. AF. TRI.	24	Thursday
3	Thursday	14	Monday	25	Friday
4	Friday	15	Tuesday	26	Saturday
5	Saturday	16	Wednesday	27	8 S. AF. TRI.
6	5 S. AF. TRI.	17	Thursday	28	Monday
7	Monday	18	Friday	29	Tuesday
8	Tuesday	19	Saturday	30	Wednesday
9	Wednesday	20	7 S. AF. TRI.	31	Thursday
10	Thursday	21	Monday		
11	Friday	22	Tuesday		

July was named in 44 B.C. for Julius Caesar. Before that the month was called Quintilius—"fifth month", March being the first month.

1

A women's swimming club is founded in Munich in 1903. One newspaper warned, presumably on behalf of the male population: "We are not yet so unnerved that we can be caught by such sensual bait".

G.W. Wallis of Sydney, Australia, learned the Aborigine Side-stroke from an aborigine at Woolooware Bay. In 1855 he took it to England where H. Gardiner used it to become the British swimming champion.

Dominion Day in Canada. The provinces were united in 1867.

The first United States postage stamps are issued, 1847.

2

July is the berry month.

3

Daisies were originally known as "day's eyes".

4   ☆

AMERICAN INDEPENDENCE DAY

> In America, the day was traditionally the most miserable day of the year for horses, tormented by all the noise and by boys who threw firecrackers at them.

The old Midsummer's Eve before the calendar changed.

Death of both John Adams and Thomas Jefferson, on the 50th anniversary of the Declaration of Independence.

The day St. Martin's remains were transferred to the cathedral in Tours. If it rains on this day, it is believed throughout Europe that there will be rain for the next twenty days.

The Statue of Liberty is presented to the United States by France in 1884.

5

P. T. Barnum born, 1810.

The first professional lion tamer was a man called "Manchester Jack". At his first performance, in 1835, he sat on the back of a very old lion and pried open the ancient beast's jaws.

6

Tennis originated in France in the middle ages. It was played indoors. Players hit a ball, made of leather stuffed with dogs hair, with either a racquet or their bare hands.

The first photograph of lightning is taken in Bohemia by Robert Haensel, 1883.

On this date in 1865 the Matterhorn is first climbed.

7

Known as "the year without a summer" in the Northeastern United States, in 1816 there was snow and a killing frost in every month and people had to wear heavy overcoats in July. People moved away for fear of starvation. There is no certain explanation for this phenomenon, but according to Professor Henry Stommel the probable cause was the eruption of the Indonesian volcano Mount Tambora. It is theorized that all the ash in the air obscured the sun's rays. The summer was extremely cold in Europe also.

The Liberty Bell cracks, 1835.

The "Burry Man" has been seen on this date every year for 600 years in South Queensbury, on the Firth of Forth. He is dressed from head to foot in a close-fitting garment covered with thistles and teazle burrs. His face cannot be seen and he goes through the streets speaking to no one.

In 1969 on this day a rhinocerous was born in Ireland for the first time.

The Feast of Lanterns in Japan occurs around this time of year.

Before the 19th century, "July" was pronounced to rhyme with "truly".

For a sting from a flying insect: Apply cucumber, honey, or yeast.

In Japan, people who visit shrines in July like to buy little cages of night-singing insects.

10

The Swiss Federal Shooting Festival is held in Lucerne every four years in mid-July.

❧

Perhaps the first shooting competition with firearms took place in South Germany in 1427. The prize for the best marksman was fifteen pairs of pants.

11

Farmers used to carry a beverage called "haymaker's switchel"—water, brown sugar, vinegar, and ginger—into the fields when haying in July and August.

❧

Those who in July are wed,
Must labor for their daily bread.

❧

12

Henry Thoreau born, 1817.

13

Bicycling through the country is a popular summer sport. The bicycle was invented by Kirkpatrick Macmillan, a Scottish blacksmith, in 1839. The first bicycle had a wooden frame with a carved horse's head on the front.

14

Bastille Day, commemorating the fall of the Bastille. Paris, 1789.

15

St. Swithin's Day. St. Swithin was a 9th-century bishop said to have caused a six-week downpour to prevent his grave from being moved 100 years after his death.

If it rains on St. Swithin's Day, some say, "St. Swithin is christening the apples".

A few drops of lavender in a closed bookcase will help prevent book mold.

16

The Muslim Era begins, 622.

The game of marbles is descended from a Roman game played with nuts. In early America, marbles were made of baked clay.

Americans used to make a "watermelon cake" that was dyed to look like a watermelon, with raisins for seeds.

A perfectly ripe watermelon
is yellow underneath.

17

In some parts of England agricultural fairs are still opened by a man walking around displaying a glove on a stick; this medieval custom guarantees that vistors may trade freely without fear of arrest.

Not tear off, but cut off, ripe beane with a knife,
    for hindering stalk of her vetive life.
So gather the lowest, leaving the top,
    shall teach thee a trick, for to double thy crop.

(The 16th-century farmer knew that if you pick beans from the bottoms of the plants your crop will be twice as big.)

18

William Makepeace Thackeray born, 1811.

chills & fever

An old remedy to get rid of ague: Make a long string of three different colored strands of yarn. Go out alone to your apple tree and tie your left hand to the tree with the string; then quickly slip your hand out of the loop and run away without looking back.

When ready to go away for vacation, weed the whole garden and soak the soil with water. Lay mulch around everything. Cut off every flower and bud; your plants will make new ones for when you come back.

In northern climates, this is the time to sow seeds for sweet William, foxgloves, pinks, and other biennials.

19

In the Northern Hemisphere, July is considered the warmest month of the year. The Romans supposed that various phenomena associated with the heat could be attributed to the rising and setting of Sirius—the Dog Star—in conjunction with the sun. Thus the period between early July and late August is known as the "dog days", even though the astronomical phenomenon with which it is associated occurs at various times of the year in different latitudes.

JULY.

1. Sunday.	17. Tuesday.
2. Monday.	18. Wednesday.
3. Tuesday.	19. Thursday.
4. Wednesday.	20. Friday.
5. Thursday.	21. Saturday.
6. Friday.	22. Sunday.
7. Saturday.	23. Monday.
8. Sunday.	24. Tuesday.
9. Monday.	25. Wednesday.
10. Tuesday.	26. Thursday.
11. Wednesday.	27. Friday.
12. Thursday	28. Saturday.
13. Friday.	29. Sunday.
14. Saturday.	30. Monday.
15. Sunday.	31. Tuesday.
16. Monday.	

"Bloomers"—invented by Mrs. Amelia Bloomer—introduced at a convention in Seneca Falls, New York, in 1848.

20

St. Margaret's Day. She was a 3rd-century saint who was saved from a dragon and is the patron saint of women in childbirth.

21

To get rid of the sting of a nettle or other vegetable: Rub the affected part with balm, rosemary, mint, or any other aromatic herb, and the smart will at once cease.

It was once believed that milk should be used to extinguish fires caused by lightning.

22

This is the day in 1284 when a musician dressed in a patched, multicolored coat—thus known as the Pied Piper—appeared in the town of Hamel, in Brunswick, struck his bargain, and exacted his famous revenge when the burghers reneged.

July.

1	5 S.AF.TRIN.	12	Thursday.	22	8 S.AF.TRIN.	
2	Monday.	13	Friday.	23	Monday.	
3	Tuesday.	14	Saturday.	24	Tuesday.	
4	Wednesday.	15	7 S.AF.TRIN	25	Wednesday.	
5	Thursday.	16	Monday.	26	Thursday.	
6	Friday.	17	Tuesday.	27	Friday.	
7	Saturday.	18	Wednesday.	28	Saturday.	
8	6 S.AF.TRIN.	19	Thursday.	29	9 S.AF.TRIN.	
9	Monday.	20	Friday.	30	Monday.	
10	Tuesday.	21	Saturday.	31	Tuesday.	
11	Wednesday.					

23

King Ludwig I of Bavaria so loved to look at pretty faces that he complained bitterly of the fashion of wearing veils that prevailed at the time. This was well known by the women of the region, who would quickly raise their veils when they saw him coming.

A Cowslip Pudding

Take two quarts of cowslip pips, pound them small, with half a pound of Naples biscuit grated, and three pints of cream. Boil these together, then beat up ten eggs with a little cream and rose water, sweeten to your taste, mix the whole well, butter a dish, and pour the ingredients in, with a little fine sugar over all, and bake it.

24

The sun enters the fifth zodiac sign of the year, Leo.

LEO ♌ The Lion.

Day of St. James the Great,
patron saint of Spain.

25

Festival of St. Christopher. French fishermen say that the floun-
der has a crooked mouth because it made faces instead of listening
when St. Christopher preached a sermon to the fishes. St. Christopher, who carried Jesus on his back across a stream, is the
patron saint of travellers.

> If you plant turnips on the twenty-fifth of July,
> You will have turnips, wet or dry.

26

The first ocean cruise offered for pleasure travelling begins at
Southampton, England. William Makepeace Thackeray was a
passenger on this four-month tour of the Mediterranean in 1844.

Australian migrant workers, or "swagmen", used to sow vegetable seeds near camping-places, so there would be food growing
there for them when they came back.

Day of St. Anne, patron saint of Canada, housewives, and miners.

27

The Festival of the Seven Sleepers. Seven young men, who did not wish to worship a statue set up by the Emperor Decius, fled to the caverns of Mount Coelius. Decius thereupon had all the caverns walled up. In 479, more than 200 years later, the seven were discovered by someone digging foundations for a stable. They were all alive, and believed they had slept only one night.

When the dew is on the grass
Rain will never come to pass.

28

Beatrix Potter born, 1866.

Last Monday in July. The swans on the River Thames between London Bridge and Henley are captured and examined for the marks that show who owns them. This custom began in the days of Elizabeth I, when a royal license was necessary to own a swan.

July.

1	Wednesday.
2	Thursday.
3	Friday.
4	Saturday.
5	5 S. AFT. TRIN.
6	Monday.
7	Tuesday.
8	Wednesday.
9	Thursday.
10	Friday.
11	Saturday.
12	6 S. AFT. TRIN.
13	Monday.
14	Tuesday.
15	Wednesday.
16	Thursday.
17	Friday.
18	Saturday.
19	7 S. AFT. TRIN.
20	Monday.
21	Tuesday.
22	Wednesday.
23	Thursday.
24	Friday.
25	Saturday.
26	8 S. AFT. TRIN.
27	Monday.
28	Tuesday.
29	Wednesday.
30	Thursday.
31	Friday.

Last Quarter.
5th day, o h. 26 m. aftern.
New Moon.
12th day, 5 h. 16 m. morn.
First Quarter.
19th day, o h. 20 m. morn.
Full Moon
27th day, 2 h. 23 m. morn.

29

Olsok Eve Festival in Norway. Bonfires are lit to commemorate St. Olaf, the king who brought Christianity to Norway in the 11th century.

Day of St. Martha, patron saint of housewives, cooks, innkeepers, and laundresses. St. Martha once had to stop her housework to overcome a dragon by sprinkling it with holy water.

30

In 1760, three of London's city gates are sold as scrap, marking the end of London as a walled city. Newgate, the last one, was burned down twenty years later by a mob.

31

Dr. Baillie's Prescription for Sick Headaches

Turkey rhubarb, finely powdered, three grains; pure soda powder dried, ten grains; sal volatile, fifteen drops. To be taken between breakfast and dinner in a glass of warm water.

Puritan mothers were advised to hang wolf fangs around their baby's neck to make teething less painful.

AOÛT

AUGUST

August.

1	Friday	17	11 S. AF. TRI.
2	Saturday	18	Monday
3	9 S. AF. TRI.	19	Tuesday
4	Bank Holid.	20	Wednesday
5	Tuesday	21	Thursday
6	Wednesday	22	Friday
7	Thursday	23	Saturday
8	Friday	24	12 S. AF. TRI.
9	Saturday	25	Monday
10	10 S. AF. TRI.	26	Tuesday
11	Monday	27	Wednesday
12	Tuesday	28	Thursday
13	Wednesday	29	Friday
14	Thursday	30	Saturday
15	Friday	31	13 S. AF. TRI.
16	Saturday		

August brings the sheaves of corn,
Then the harvest home is borne.

1

In the old Roman calendar, this, the sixth month, was named Sextilis. Because of the auspicious events that occurred during it, Augustus chose to confer his name upon this month instead of his birth month.

Known in Britain and in early colonial times as Lammas Day. This was the end of the farming season in Britain, where the harvest starts earlier than it does in the United States. It was the farmers' thanksgiving time, and it was the American Thanksgiving time until 1863.

American families would take the first loaf of bread from the new grain to church to be blessed by the minister. The word "Lammas" was originally "Loaf Mass".

Institution in 1469 of the French order of knighthood—the Order of St. Michael. The thirty-six knights could be degraded only for heresy, treason, or cowardice.

New London Bridge opened by King William IV and Queen Adelaide in 1831. Old London Bridge had been built in 1209 and carried a nearly continuous row of four-story buildings, interrupted only by an open area used for jousting in medieval times.

Swiss Confederation Day. Commemorates creation of the Swiss confederation in 1291 for defense against the Austrians.

To make water cold for summer: Let the jar, pitcher, or vessel used for water be surrounded with one or more folds of coarse cotton, to be constantly wet. The evaporation of the water will carry off the heat from the inside and reduce it to a freezing point.

London, 1865. Publication of *Alice's Adventures in Wonderland* by Lewis Carroll; only forty-eight copies were sold.

The first street letter boxes in the United States are installed in 1858 in Boston and New York.

August and March are the times to plant evergreens.

When the grass is dry at morning light
Look for rain before the night.

August.

1 Wednesday.	11 Saturday.	22 Wednesday
2 Thursday.	12 11 S. AF. TRI.	23 Thursday.
3 Friday.	13 Monday.	24 Friday.
4 Saturday.	14 Tuesday.	25 Saturday.
5 10 S. AF. TRI.	15 Wednesday.	26 13 S. AF. TRI.
6 Bank Holid.	16 Thursday.	27 Monday.
7 Tuesday.	17 Friday.	28 Tuesday.
8 Wednesday.	18 Saturday.	29 Wednesday.
9 Thursday	19 12 S. AF. TRI.	30 Thursday.
10 Friday.	20 Monday.	31 Friday.
	21 Tuesday.	

5

A feast in Rome, that includes a shower of blossoms, commemorates a snow shower on this day in the 3rd century that outlined the shape of a basilica. The Day of Our Lady of the Snows.

6

Nasturtium sandwiches. Use ⅔ flowers, ⅓ leaves on buttered thin slices of bread.

To Make Rose Brandy

Fill a jar loosely with fresh rose-petals, then add enough white brandy to fill the jar. Every day strain the brandy, throw out the rose petals, and put in new ones, until the rose season is over.

7

Peach leaves steeped in brandy make an excellent seasoning for custards and puddings.

AUGUST.

1. Wednesday.
2. Thursday.
3. Friday.
4. Saturday.
5. SUNDAY.
6. Monday.
7. Tuesday.
8. Wednesday.
9. Thursday.
10. Friday.
11. Saturday.
12. SUNDAY.
13. Monday.
14. Tuesday.
15. Wednesday

16. Thursday.
17. Friday,
18. Saturday.
19. SUNDAY.
20. Monday.
21. Tuesday.
22. Wednesday.
23. Thursday.
24. Friday.
25. Saturday.
26. SUNDAY.
27. Monday.
28. Tuesday.
29. Wednesday.
30. Thursday.
31. Friday.

Fruit spots are removed from white and fast-coloured cottons by the use of chloride of soda. Commence by cold-soaping the article, then touch the spot with a hair-pencil or feather dipped in the chloride, dipping it immediately into cold water to prevent the texture of the article from being injured.

Izaak Walton born, 1593.

In August, trees, vines, and perennials stop growing and begin to get ready for winter.

Where Ivie embraceth the tree verie sore
kill Ivie, or else tree will addle [grow] no more.

According to an old New England be-lief, boy babies should sleep without nightcaps as soon as they have any hair.

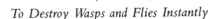

11

To Destroy Wasps and Flies Instantly

Wasps and flies may be killed very fast, by dipping a feather in a little sweet oil, and touching their backs with it; they will instantly die. When intent on the fruit, and half-buried in the excavations they have made, they are easily come at, and are not apt to fly about. Insects of different kinds are easily killed by oil; it closes up the lateral pores by which they breathe.

QUAGGA

12

The quagga in Amsterdam's Zoo Artis dies in 1883. This was the last quagga (a zebra-like animal) in the world.

The Saxon name for August was *Weod Monath*, which means "weed-month"

Goldenrod is not really the hay-fever-allergy culprit it is believed to be: Ragweed makes more people sneeze. Goldenrod is a native American flower, which used to be exported to Europe, where it was prized for medicinal properties.

Before dandelions became weeds, they were cultivated on purpose. People ate the leaves as a vegetable and ground the roots for a coffee-like drink.

13

Vegetables should be gathered in the cool of the morning or evening. If gathered when the sun is upon them, they are sure to be tough and discolored.

Great care must be taken to gather fruit for preserves on a dry day; otherwise it will never keep.

Dry August and warm doth harvest no harm.

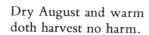

14

Bourbon, a corn whiskey, is an American invention. Legend has it that the idea of flavoring whiskey by storing it in smoked wood was discovered by accident when an oaken whiskey barrel was struck by lightning.

15

Sir Walter Scott born, 1771.

Taught by the Indians, early Americans made brooms of split birch. Twig-brooms, used in Europe, were seldom seen in the New World.

Assumption Day. A major holiday in Roman Catholic countries and the beginning of summer holidays for many people in Europe.

Grass should not be cut too short in midsummer. Grass roots need some shade from the hot sun.

Tivoli, the pleasure garden of Copenhagen, opens, 1843.

16

The Alaskan gold rush starts on this date in 1896.

17

The Use of Garlic Against Moles, Grubs, and Snails

Moles are such enemies to the smell of garlic, that, in order to get rid of these troublesome and destructive guests, it is sufficient to introduce a few heads of garlic into their subterraneous walks. It is likewise employed with success against grubs and snails.

When leaves show their undersides.
Be very sure that rain betides.

The U. S. Weather Bureau has three sets of people's names for hurricanes originating in each area. Every four years they start over again with the first set of names, except in the Atlantic where the cycle is ten years. The names of major hurricanes are not used again for at least ten years. Now they use both male and female names.

In the 19th century, people bought "snake balls", pieces of stone or bone that were supposed to draw out the poison when placed on a snakebite.

18

American plant patent #1 is granted in 1931 to Henry F. Bosenberg of New Brunswick, New Jersey, for New Dawn, a rose that blooms repeatedly instead of only once.

19

Whoever wed in August be,
Many a change is sure to see.

In Germany it is said: men who hate cats will never get a wife. This derives from the old Germanic folk belief that the wildcat was the favorite animal of Freya, the goddess of love and marriage.

20

Until the 17th century, the country people of Europe usually made weekly visits to the bathhouses in the nearby towns. With the advent of flax-growing and the use of washable linen underwear, the frequency of these visits diminished drastically.

21

Easy Method of Preserving Animal Food Sweet for Several Days in the Height of Summer

Veal, mutton, beef, or venison may be kept for nine or ten days perfectly sweet and good, in the heat of summer, by lightly covering the same with bran, and hanging it in a high and windy room; therefore a cupboard full of small holes, or a wire safe, so as the wind may have a passage through, is recommended to be placed in such a room, to keep away the flies.

22

To Preserve Meat by Treacle

This experiment has been successfully tried in the following manner. A gentleman put a piece of beef into treacle, and turned it often. At the end of a month he ordered it to be washed and boiled, and had the pleasure to find it quite good, and more pleasant than the same piece would have been in salt for that time.

23

An old almanac lists the following as fertilizers: bones, woolen rags, fish, leather, soapsuds, brine, lime, mud from the swamps and ponds, straw, ferns, rotten wood, shells, ashes.

24

On the fourth Sunday in August, dairymen of Vissoie, Switzerland, return from the Alpine pastures, where they have spent the summer with their cattle, and present their priest with the first cheese of the season.

If the twenty-fourth of August be fair and clear,
Then hope for a prosperous Autumn that year.

VIRGO   ♍   *The Virgin.*

The sun enters the sixth zodiac sign of the year, Virgo.

St. Bartholemew's Day. It was once a rule in parts of Germany that innkeepers must provide fresh cider for their guests on this day or lose their right to sell drinks in the following year.

Cuckoo, cuckoo,
What do you do?
In April
I open my bill;
In May
I sing night and day;
In June
I change my tune;
In July,
Away I fly;
In August
Away I must.

25

BRITISH SUMMER HOLIDAY

Day of St. Louis, patron saint of France and of barbers.

26

The typewriter is patented in 1843.

❧

Olivier van Noort, the first Dutchman to have circled the globe, returns in 1601 with one ship and forty-five crew members. He had left in 1598 with four ships and 248 crewmen.

27

In 1890 Miss Zee Gayton set out to walk from San Francisco to New York, which she did in 226 days.

28

The first motor tour was made in Germany in 1888 by Bertha Benz, who took her children to visit relatives. Her husband was the inventor of the car she was driving. Drinkers at an inn where they stopped in the Black Forest quarreled about whether the automobile was powered by clockwork or by a supernatural source.

"Jonny-cake" is an authentic American dish; the name comes from "journey-cake"—cakes to take on a trip. To be completely authentic, jonny-cake should be made of cornmeal from Narragansett, Rhode Island.

29

In North America, when the katydid begins to sing, the first frost is due in six weeks.

30

The Day of St. Fiacre. Horse-drawn cabs in France are called *fiacres* to this day because of a taxi business started in Paris at the Hôtel St. Fiacre.

31

Bill of Fare for a Picnic for 40 Persons

A joint of cold roast beef, a joint of cold boiled beef, 2 ribs of lamb, 2 shoulders of lamb, 4 roast fowls, 2 roast ducks, 1 ham, 1 tongue, 2 veal-and-ham pies, 2 pigeon pies, 6 medium-sized lobsters, 1 piece of collared calf's head, 18 lettuces, 6 baskets of salad, 6 cucumbers.

Stewed fruit well sweetened, and put into glass bottles well corked; 3 or 4 dozen plain pastry biscuits to eat with the stewed fruit, 2 dozen fruit turnovers, 4 dozen cheesecakes, 2 cold cabinet puddings in moulds, 2 blancmanges in moulds, a few jam puffs, 1 large cold plum-pudding (this must be good), a few baskets of fresh fruit, 3 dozen plain biscuits, a piece of cheese, 6 lbs. of butter (this, of course, includes the butter for tea), 4 quartern loaves of household bread, 3 dozen rolls, 6 loaves of tin bread (for tea), 2 plain plum cakes, 2 pound cakes, 2 sponge cakes, a tin of mixed biscuits, ½ lb. of tea.

SEPTEMBRE

SEPTEMBER

September.

1	Monday	16	Tuesday
2	Tuesday	17	Wednesday
3	Wednesday	18	Thursday
4	Thursday	19	Friday
5	Friday	20	Saturday
6	Saturday	21	16 S. af. Tri.
7	14 S. af. Tri.	22	Monday
8	Monday	23	Tuesday
9	Tuesday	24	Wednesday
10	Wednesday	25	Thursday
11	Thursday	26	Friday
12	Friday	27	Saturday
13	Saturday	28	17 S. af. Tri.
14	15 S. af. Tri.	29	Monday
15	Monday	30	Tuesday

September blow soft
Till the fruit's in the loft.

1

Emma Nutt, the first female telephone operator, begins work in Boston, 1878.

This is the beginning of the oyster season. At Colchester in England, a toast is traditionally drunk to the Queen in a thimbleful of gin, and a "pinch of gingerbread" is served.

Oysters should be eaten only in months that have the letter "R" in their names, which excludes the warm months. September is the first oyster month after the "no-R" summer months.

In the 19th century, people could ship each other barrels of oysters as presents, even if they lived as far as a month's journey away: Oysters were packed in barrels of salted water, which was changed every day, and cornmeal was scattered through the barrel.

2

Belgium's most famous bell, Klokke Roelant, is consecrated in 1660 in Ghent. It weighs 13,310 pounds (6,050 kg).

The Great Fire of London, 1666

3

Marry in September's shine,
Your living will be rich and fine.

4

The founding of Los Angeles, 1781.

5

Born this day in 1638, the future Louis XIV of France—with two lower front teeth.

6

September.

1 Tuesday.
2 Wednesday.
3 Thursday.
4 Friday]
5 Saturday.
6 14 S. AFT. TRIN.
7 Monday.
8 Tuesday.
9 Wednesday.
10 Thursday.
11 Friday.
12 Saturday.
13 15 S. AFT. TRIN.
14 Monday.
15 Tuesday.
16 Wednesday.
17 Thursday.
18 Friday.
19 Saturday.
20 16 S. AFT. TRIN.
21 Monday.
22 Tuesday.
23 Wednesday.
24 Thursday.
25 Friday.
26 Saturday.
27 17 S. AFT. TRIN.
28 Monday.
29 Tu. Mich. Day.
30 Wednesday.

Last Quarter.
2nd day, 5 h. 15 m. morn.
New Moon.
8th day, 8 h. 43 m. aftern.
First Quarter.
16th day, 6 h. 15 m. morn.
Full Moon.
24th day, 7 h. 55 m. morn.

German Furniture Gloss

Cut in small pieces a quarter of a pound of yellow wax; and, melting it in a pipkin, add an ounce of well-pounded colophony, or black rosin. The wax and colophony being both melted, pour in, by degrees, quite warm, two ounces of oil or spirits of turpentine. When the whole is thoroughly mixed, pour it into a tin or earthen pot, and keep it covered for use. The method of applying it to the furniture, which must be first well dusted and cleaned, is by spreading a little of this composition on a piece of woollen cloth, and well rubbing the wood with it; and, in a few days the gloss will be as firm and fast as varnish.

7

Elizabeth I born, 1533.

8

The first Monday in September is American Labor Day.

September is back-to-school time.

A boy who wears new clothes to school in England would be reminded by the other boys that "pride must be pinched". They will pinch him and say, "A nip for new".

In early America it was the practice for the schoolteacher—usually a man—to "board around" at different pupils' houses. This was an inexpensive way of living and allowed the teacher to become acquainted with his pupils.

10

There is a harmony
In Autumn, and a lustre in its sky,
Which thro' the Summer is not heard or seen.
Shelley

September.

1	Tuesday	16	Wednesday
2	Wednesday	17	Thursday
3	Thursday	18	Friday
4	Friday	19	Saturday
5	Saturday	20	17 S.A.TRIN.
6	15 S.A.TRIN.	21	Monday
7	Monday	22	Tuesday
8	Tuesday	23	Wednesday
9	Wednesday	24	Thursday
10	Thursday	25	Friday
11	Friday	26	Saturday
12	Saturday	27	18 S.A.TRIN.
13	16 S.A.TRIN.	28	Monday
14	Monday	29	ST MICHAEL
15	Tuesday	30	Wednesday

Names of American quilt patterns:
Four-Square, Nine-Square, Rising Sun,
Log Cabin, Star of Bethlehem, Tree of
Life, Jacob's Ladder, Rose of Sharon,
Whig Rose, Yankee Pride, 54–40 or
Fight, Lincoln's Platform, Air Castle,
Lovers' Links, Orange Peel.

11

ROSH HASHANAH

The Jewish New Year. Honey is one of the things that is eaten on
this holiday, as an omen for a sweet year. In Jewish tradition,
Rosh Hashanah is the day the world was created, and the civil
calendar begins here. It is the beginning of a ten-day period of
spiritual renewal.

The Jewish calendar is based on the
phases of the moon. In ancient times,
official witnesses were sent out to watch
for the appearance of the new moon,
which would be the signal for the start
of a new month. When two witnesses
reported seeing the new moon, lines of
bonfires would be lighted on hilltops to
tell the people that the next month had
begun.

12

The jam- and jelly-making season extends from the first days of July to the end of September, beginning with strawberries and ending with apples and plums.

Set strawberries, wife,
I love them for life.
Plant Respe and rose,
And such as those.

Set herbes some more,
for winter store.

13

Fruit gathered too timely will taste of the wood,
  will shrink and be bitter, and seldom proove good.
So fruit that is shaken, or beat off a tree,
  with bruising in falling, soon faultie will be.

14

Daredevil Charles Blondin crosses Niagara Falls in 1860 walking on stilts along a rope. Young Edward, Prince of Wales, watches.

15

According to a 19th century account, Vincent Lunardi makes the first sustained English ascent in 1784 and becomes a national sensation, announcing "In the air balloon to distant realms I fly/And leave the creeping world to sink and die".

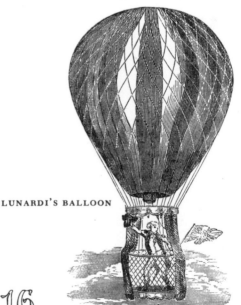

LUNARDI'S BALLOON

MAYFLOWER

16

In 1620 the Mayflower sails from Plymouth, England.

O wild West Wind, thou breath of Autumn's being,
Thou, from whose unseen presence the leaves dead
Are driven, like ghosts from an enchanter fleeing.

Shelley

The American pie is perhaps the most ridiculed of all dishes. It has, however, great popularity and undoubted merits. Were the crust, especially the under one, always right, it would remove the most salient point of criticism. The tart pies, made with puffpaste, are a temptation to the most fastidious taste. The mince pie, probably the most indigestible of all, is the one universally accepted as a treat, and seldom refused by the scoffer.

Pies have their seasons, like other good things, the apple pie being the only one served the year round. The berries and fruits, each one in their time, make most acceptable and delicious pies and tarts, while rhubarb introduces the spring, and pumpkin announces the autumn. In this day of canned and dried fruits the season need not be so strictly observed, but fresh fruits will always be preferable to preserved ones,

17

St. Lambert's Day. On this day in the town of Rupertwinkel it was once permissable to thrash an enemy with impunity while the churchbell sounded.

18

Now is the time to cut the dead flowers off flowering plants. The annuals will bloom again before the frost. The perennials must be prevented from wasting their energy by making seeds.

Clean up the garden at the end of September before it gets too cold. Pull up the annuals, chop down perennial stalks, weed thoroughly.

19

At Versailles, 1783, Louis XVI and Marie Antoinette watch the ascent of the Montgolfier brothers' first (hot-air) balloon. It carried a sheep, a duck, and a rooster, the first "manned" flight.

The first appearance of a Mickey Mouse cartoon, *Steamboat Willie,* in 1928.

LIBRA   ♎   *The Balance.*

The sun enters the seventh zodiac sign of the year, Libra.

20

YOM KIPPUR

The Day of Atonement, the most holy day in the Jewish year, when people fast and pray and seek forgiveness.

❧

An English officer near Calcutta notes a quantity of live fish falling in a rain shower in 1839. (Incidents of frog, rat, and insect showers, probably caused by whirlwinds or waterspouts, are also recorded.)

In the fall, when it starts to get cold, mice look for warm houses in which to spend the winter. The word "mouse" comes from the Sanskrit word *mus,* which means "thief".

21

The first issue of a daily newspaper in America, *The Pennsylvania Evening Post and Daily Advertiser.* Philadelphia, 1793.

If geese appear early in the South, a hard winter is coming in the North.

The full moon in September nearest the autumn equinox is known as the harvest moon. Because of its position in relation to Earth, it seems to be very big and to rise very slowly.

Ceres, the Roman grain goddess, was worshipped at this time of year. She was known in ancient Britain variously as:

> The Harvest Queen
> The Kern Baby
> The Corn Baby
> The Kern Doll
> The Ivy Girl
> The Neck
> The Mare

Set hive on a plank (not too low by the ground)
   where herbe with the flowers may compas it round:
And boordes to defend it from north and north east,
   from showers and rubbish, from vermin and beast.

AUTUMN

AUTUMN.

The morrow was a bright September morn;
The earth was beautiful as if new-born;
There was that nameless splendor everywhere,
The wild exhilaration in the air,
Which makes the passers in the city street
Congratulate each other as they meet.

Longfellow

22

The sun crosses the equator—the autumnal equinox.

The biggest banquet ever is served by M. Loubet, President of the Republic, to all the 2,200 mayors of France and their deputies in the Tuileries gardens, Paris, in 1900.

23

Lady bug, Lady bug, fly away home,
Your house is on fire and your children will burn.

In Europe, the hop vines were burned in the fall after harvest to get rid of the aphids. Ladybug larvae eat aphids, so people recited this rhyme to warn them away from the fires.

131

24

The Feast of Ingathering—Harvest Home. In old times the grain last cut was brought home in a cart, topped by a sheaf gaily dressed in the form of a figure. The cart was followed by a procession of singing and dancing farmers, and the rejoicing was concluded with a feast.

25

SUKKOTH

Sukkoth, the festival of booths, or tabernacles, is a Jewish autumn holiday. Families traditionally build small sheds covered with branches in memory of the Israelites' shelters in the wilderness.

According to legend, the weather for the coming year could be predicted by watching the chimney smoke on Sukkoth: If it blows to the North, the poor will be happy, the rich disappointed; rain will be plentiful, food cheap; if to the South, it will be a dry year, with high prices; to the East, the best possible; to the West, famine.

Until 1845 at Kiddermister, Worcestershire, a "lawless hour" was observed by the townspeople, who assembled in the main street and threw cabbage stalks at each other from three until four P.M. At four, a new bailiff would appear in a procession. As the officials marched through town, the rich people would throw apples at them from their windows.

26

Where stones be too manie, annoying thy land,
   make servant come home with a stone in his hand.
By daily so dooing, have plentie ye shall,
   both handsome for paving and good for a wall.

27

This is when the old-time farmer brought home brush for cooking fires, shed roofing, and the cow's bed.

28

Some believe that to catch a leaf as it falls from a tree brings either a wish or a day of good luck.

Horseflies bite more when rain is coming.

29

MICHAELMAS

St. Michael's Day or Michaelmas—the oldest of the "Angel" festivals. St. Michael is regarded as the protector against the devil and the guide to heaven. This autumn holiday marks the beginning of the dark time of the year.

Michaelmas is one of the four days upon which quarterly rent is commonly paid. Goose is usually eaten at dinner. Magistrates were traditionally appointed on this day, and rulers were propitiated with the gift of a goose.

By tradition, one may sleep late on St. Michael's Day:

> Nature requires five,
>   Custom gives seven;
> Laziness takes nine,
>   And Michaelmas eleven.

30

It is believed that all the blackberries in the world are poisoned on this day, the devil having put his foot on them the night before.

OCTOBRE

OCTOBER

October.

1	Wednesday	12	19 S. AF. TRI.	23	Thursday
2	Thursday	13	Monday	24	Friday
3	Friday	14	Tuesday	25	Saturday
4	Saturday	15	Wednesday	26	21 S. AF. TRI.
5	18 S. AF. TRI.	16	Thursday	27	Monday
6	Monday	17	Friday	28	Tuesday
7	Tuesday	18	Saturday	29	Wednesday
8	Wednesday	19	20 S. AF. TRI.	30	Thursday
9	Thursday	20	Monday	31	Friday
10	Friday	21	Tuesday		
11	Saturday	22	Wednesday		

Season of mists and mellow fruitfulness,
   Close bosom-friend of the maturing sun;
Conspiring with him how to load and bless
   With fruit the vines that round the thatch-eaves run;
To bend with apples the mossed cottage-trees,
   And fill all fruit with ripeness to the core;
     To swell the gourd, and plump the hazel shells
   With a sweet kernel; to set budding more,
And still more, later flowers for the bees,
Until they think warm days will never cease,
    For Summer has o'er-brimmed their clammy cells.

Keats

October 1 and May 1 are the most popular days for moving into new houses in the United States.

First agricultural fair in America held in Pittsfield, Massachusetts, 1810.

A German provincial ordinance of 1792 was as specific as it was hard. It prescribed which hours cattle were to be in their stalls and which they should be in pasture. It set the amounts of daily wages; an employer who paid more was fined, an employee who accepted more was given eight days at hard labor on bread and water plus twelve lashes a day.

Eleanora Duse born in 1859, when her parents were on tour with a theatrical company in Lombardy. She was carried to her christening in a gilt theatrical property box.

4

Day of St. Francis of Assisi.

5

There is an old American belief that you could get rid of an infestation of rats by writing them a letter and persuading them to go elsewhere. The letter should be rolled up and put into one of their holes. Following is an example of such a letter dated October 5, 1888. A writer of the time assures us that as a result of this letter "the number of the pests had been considerably diminished".

Messrs. Rats and Co.,—Having taken quite a deep interest in your welfare in regard to your winter quarters I thought I would drop you a few lines which might be of some considerable benefit to you in the future seeing that you have pitched your winter quarters at the summer residence of ✷ ✷ ✷ No. 1 Seaview Street, I wish to inform you that you will be very much disturbed during cold winter months as I am expecting to be at work through all parts of the house, shall take down ceilings, take up

floors, and clean out every substance that would serve to make you comfortable, likewise there will be nothing left for you to feed on, as I shall remove every eatable substance; so you had better take up your abode elsewhere. I will here refer you to the farm of ★ ★ ★No. 6 Incubator Street, where you will find a splendid cellar well filled with vegetations of (all) kinds besides a shed leading to a barn, with a good supply of grain, where you can live snug and happy. Shall do you no harm if you heed to my advice; but if not, shall employ "Rough on Rats".

Yours,

6

Walnut vinegar. Put green walnut shells into a brine of salt and water strong enough to float an egg. Remove after ten or twelve days and lay them in the sun for a week. Then put them in a jar and put boiling vinegar on them. In a week or so pour off the vinegar, boil it, and pour it back. This will be good to eat in about a month and is especially nice with meat.

7

Verjuice

Gather some ripe crab apples, and lay them in a heap to sweat; then throw away the stalks and decayed fruit, and having mashed the apples express the juice. A cyder or wine-press will be useful for this purpose. Strain it, and in a month it will be ready. It is the best simple substitute for lemon-juice that can be found, and answers still better in place of sorrel.

To get clivias to bloom at Christmas-time, start leaving them dry in early October, then water them heavily in late December. This imitates the seasonal drought/rain conditions of their natural environment in South Africa.

Leif Ericson Day. The landing of the Vikings in the New World in the year 1000 is celebrated by Americans of Scandinavian descent in Wisconsin and Minnesota.

Giuseppe Verdi born, 1813.

To Make Indian Ink

Put six lighted wicks into a dish of oil; hang an iron or tin concave cover over it so as to receive all the smoke; when there is a sufficient quantity of soot set-tled to the cover, then take it off gently with a feather upon a sheet of paper, and mix it up with gum tragacanth to a pro-per consistence.

OCTOBER.

1.	Monday.	16.	Tuesday.
2.	Tuesday.	17.	Wednesday.
3.	Wednesday.	18.	Thursday.
4.	Thursday.	19.	Friday,
5.	Friday.	20.	Saturday.
6.	Saturday.	21.	Sunday.
7.	Sunday.	22.	Monday.
8.	Monday.	23.	Tuesday.
9.	Tuesday.	24.	Wednesday.
10.	Wednesday.	25.	Thursday.
11.	Thursday.	26.	Friday.
12.	Friday.	27.	Saturday.
13.	Saturday.	28.	Sunday.
14.	Sunday.	29.	Monday.
15.	Monday	30.	Tuesday.
		31.	Wednesday.

A 24-carat diamond set in the floor of the Capitol Building in Havana is the starting point for measuring all distances in Cuba.

Old Michaelmas Day. At Bishop's Stortford, Hertfordshire, this was known as "ganging day". Young men would grab anyone they met and bump him or her against a tree, gatepost, or another person. Nice women usually stayed home.

11

William Bowler of London made a special hat for William Coke to protect his head from overhead branches while hunting. This was the first "bowler".

12

Columbus Day, commemorating his first sighting of the New World in 1492.

President Theodore Roosevelt renames the "Executive Mansion" "The White House", 1901.

13

If cornhusks cling tight to the cob a hard winter is coming.

The straw and the ear to have bigness and length,
    betokeneth land to be good and in strength.
If eare be but short, and the strawe be but small,
    it signifieth bareness and barren withall.

14

An apple-tree puts to shame all the men and
women that have attempted to dress since
the world began.

H. W. Beecher

October is the apple harvest month.
There are many beliefs, sayings, and
games associated with apples. The
game of bobbing for apples in a tub
originated at apple harvest celebrations;
if you throw an apple peel over your
shoulder, the letter it forms will be the
initial of your future husband; stick two
apple seeds on your cheeks and name
each one for a suitor—the one that
sticks longest loves you most.

Apples shouldn't touch each other in storage. Marble shelves are
especially good for keeping apples.

To preserve apples: Dry a glazed jar and put a few small stones in
the bottom. Fill the jar with apples and cover it with a piece of
wood that fits the top exactly, spreading fresh mortar over it.

15

It is bad luck to peel peaches, pears, or apples alone.

American farmers used to make a pear cider called "perry".

A waistcoat is worn for the first time, in 1666, by Charles II of England. According to Samuel Pepys, it was "a long cassocke close to the body, of black cloth and pink white silk under it".

16

PUMPKIN PIES

Pare a small pumpkin, about four pounds, and take out the seeds. Steam till soft, and strain through a colander.

Beat in three eggs, three tablespoonfuls of molasses, two tablespoonfuls of ground cinnamon, one of ginger, two teaspoonfuls of salt, and two quarts of hot milk. If more sweetening is needed add a little sugar. Bake with an under crust only. This receipt will make five pies.

Onions keep best roped and hung up in a dry cold room.

Small cabbages, laid on a stone floor before the frost sets in, will blanch and be very fine, after many weeks' keeping.

17

Never was a newspaper so heavy as this 1965 Sunday's *New York Times*. It had 946 pages and weighed 7½ pounds (3.4 kg).

Wait until any possibility of Indian Summer is over to plant tulip bulbs.

Clear moon, frost soon.

18

At the Harvest Moon in China, women celebrate a moon festival, setting up tables bearing a picture of the moon, and representations of a rabbit and a pine tree.

In the month of October in Peru, people wear purple to commemorate a black artist of the 17th century, known as Señor de los Milagros, who painted a picture believed to have saved a building from an earthquake on this day.

If the moon shows a silver shield,
Be not afraid to reap your field.

19

If in October you do marry,
Love will come, but riches tarry.

The full moon in October is known as the Hunters' Moon.

October.

1	Thursday	17	Saturday
2	Friday	18	21 S.A.TRIN.
3	Saturday	19	Monday
4	19 S.A.TRIN.	20	Tuesday
5	Monday	21	Wednesday
6	Tuesday	22	Thursday
7	Wednesday	23	Friday
8	Thursday	24	Saturday
9	Friday	25	22 S.A.TRIN.
10	Saturday	26	Monday
11	20 S.A.TRIN.	27	Tuesday
12	Monday	28	Wednesday
13	Tuesday	29	Thursday
14	Wednesday	30	Friday
15	Thursday	31	Saturday
16	Friday		

20

Herbs and plants used for dyeing cloth:

YELLOW: alder leaves, apple bark, aster flowers, bayberry leaves, camomile flowers, horse chestnut husks and leaves, catnip plant, peach bark.

GREEN: chess wheat, lily of the valley leaves, nettle roots, oak bark, parsley.

BLUE: blueberries, elderberries; indigo plant, larkspur flowers.

PURPLE: black cherry bark and roots, cockleburr plant, dandelion root, grape.

RED: beetroot, bloodroot, dogwood root, hollyhock flowers and leaves, madder root, St. John's wort flowers and leaves.

21

Day of St. Ursula, the patron saint of brides. In the early 18th century, France sent shiploads of wives to lonely Louisiana settlers. Each bride brought a chest containing a blanket, four sheets, two pairs of stockings, six headdresses, and a pelisse. Their arrival in New Orleans was celebrated with parades in honor of St. Ursula.

October.

1 Monday.	11 Thursday.	22 Monday.
2 Tuesday.	12 Friday.	23 Tuesday.
3 Wednesday.	13 Saturday.	24 Wednesday.
4 Thursday.	14 20 S. af. Tri.	25 Thursday.
5 Friday.	15 Monday.	26 Friday.
6 Saturday.	16 Tuesday.	27 Saturday.
7 19 S. af. Tri.	17 Wednesday.	28 22 S. af. Tri.
8 Monday.	18 Thursday.	29 Monday.
9 Tuesday.	19 Friday.	30 Tuesday.
10 Wednesday.	20 Saturday.	31 Wednesday.
	21 21 S. af. Tri.	

22

Sarah Bernhardt born, 1845.

23

Cider making is the northern substitute for wine making. This is how it is done the old way: The apples are gathered, left out to mellow, ground in the cider mill; the pulp or potage is pressed in the cider press. The resulting juice is kept in lightly corked casks until spring, and then, with bungs tightly fixed, aged for (ideally) eighteen months to two years.

Cider is made from bruised apples, apple juice from undamaged apples.

In Kentucky there is a folk belief that if you can break an apple in half with your bare hands you can marry anybody you want. You can also get your choice of spouse if you can eat a crab apple without frowning.

Some names of apples: Golden Russett, Tolman Sweet, Snow Apple, Ribston, Normandy, Baldwin, Ben Davis, Cortland, Delicious, Early McIntosh, Golden Delicious, Grimes Golden, Gravenstein, Jonathan, Lodi, Macoun, McIntosh, Newtown Pippin, Northern Spy, Cox's Orange Pippin, Granny Smith, Worcester, Nonpareil, Keswick, Wealthy, Yellow Transparent, York Imperial, Spygold.

24

SCORPIO   ♏   The Scorpion.

The sun enters the eighth zodiac sign of the year, Scorpio.

25

St. Crispin's Day. Crispin and his brother Chrispinian are the patron saints of shoemakers, who used to hold great celebrations on this day.

October.

1 Thursday.
2 Friday.
3 Saturday.
4 18 S. AFT. TRIN.
5 Monday.
6 Tuesday.
7 Wednesday.
8 Thursday.
9 Friday.
10 Saturday.
11 19 S. AFT. TRIN.
12 Monday.
13 Tuesday.
14 Wednesday.
15 Thursday.
16 Friday.
17 Saturday.
18 20 S. AFT. TRIN.
19 Monday.
20 Tuesday.
21 Wednesday.
22 Thursday.
23 Friday.
24 Saturday.
25 21 S. AFT. TRIN.
26 Monday.
27 Tuesday.
28 Wednesday.
29 Thursday.
30 Friday.
31 Saturday.

Last Quarter.
1st day, 11 h. 29 m. morn.
New Moon.
8th day, 7 h. 31 m. morn.
First Quarter.
16th day, 1 h. 21 m. morn.
Full Moon.
23rd day, 9 h. 23 m. aftern.
Last Quarter.
30th day, 5 h. 58 m. aftern.

Punch was brought from India in the 17th century. Its name derives from the Hindustani word for "five", signifying the number of ingredients used (spirits, water, sugar, lemon, and spice).

In 1694, Admiral Russell, commander of the British Mediterranean fleet, uses 4 hogsheads of brandy, one pipe of Malaga wine, 20 gallons of lime-juice, 2500 lemons, 13 hundredweight of fine white sugar, 5 lbs. grated nutmegs, 300 toasted biscuits, and 8 hogsheads of water to make a punch at Alicante, Spain. A canopy was put over the punch to retard evaporation, and a shipboy rowed around in the fountain to assist in serving.

The old custom of floating toasted bread in the punch explains the tradition of drinking toasts. Supposedly, a famous beauty was taking the waters at Bath (attired in a modest bathing costume) and several admirers drank her health with her bathwater. One of them offered to jump in, remarking that he liked the liquor, but would prefer the toast (i.e. the lady).

In ancient Greece, for the festival of the Thesmophoria, women built bowers of plants and sat on the ground to encourage corn to grow and ensure their own fertility.

26

The Saxons called October *Win Monath*—time for making wine.

27

In Germany, the Oktoberfest is a month of feasting. This custom was begun in Bavaria in 1810 to celebrate the wedding of the future King Ludwig I.

Beginning of Book-Reading Week in Japan, when people are encouraged to stay home in the evening and read books.

28

Households smell like cinnamon at pie-baking time. In the Middle Ages, cinnamon was so widely believed to have curative powers that a common question was, "Why does a man die who can get cinnamon to eat?"

29

Late October is the time to buy paper-white narcissus bulbs to force for Christmas: They take six weeks.

30

Put Christmas cactus away in a cool, dark place for fourteen hours a day for six weeks at this time of year if you want flowers at Christmas-time.

31

HALLOWEEN

There are many legends to explain the tricking custom of Halloween. According to one, November 1 was the Druidic feast of the Lord of Death before it became All Saint's Day. Some people became frightened at this time, and some of those who didn't played pranks on them.

There is a Scottish belief that people born on Halloween have second sight.

To frighten witches, people used to hollow out a turnip, carve a face on it, and put a candle inside. This is how the Halloween pumpkin custom began.

NOVEMBER

November.

1	Saturday	11	Tuesday	21	Friday
2	22 S. AF. TRI.	12	Wednesday	22	Saturday
3	Monday	13	Thursday	23	25 S. AF. TRI.
4	Tuesday	14	Friday	24	Monday
5	Wednesday	15	Saturday	25	Tuesday
6	Thursday	16	24 S. AF. TRI.	26	Wednesday
7	Friday	17	Monday	27	Thursday
8	Saturday	18	Tuesday	28	Friday
9	23 S. AF. TRI.	19	Wednesday	29	Saturday
10	Monday	20	Thursday	30	1 S. IN ADV.

November's sky is chill and drear,
November's leaf is red and sear.

Walter Scott

1

November was known by the Saxons as *Wint Monath*—the wind month.

The great Lisbon earthquake and tidal wave of 1755.

All Saint's Day. This holiday commemorates those who led saintly lives but have not been formally recognized as saints.

2

All Soul's Day. There was an old belief that on this day unhappy souls returned to their former homes. It was the custom to keep kitchens warm and leave food on the table overnight for the benefit of visiting spirits.

3

No warmth, no cheerfulness, no healthful ease
No comfortable feel in any member—
No shade, no shine, no butterflies, no bees
No fruits, no flowers, no leaves, no birds.
November!

Thomas Hood

4

Ivy should be covered with dead leaves unless snow can be counted on to blanket it for the winter.

5

Guy Fawkes' Day. In England, bonfires are lit and boys carry around an effigy of Guy Fawkes in memory of the day in 1605 when he was discovered in the basement of Parliament getting ready to blow it up, just as the King was about to make his opening speech. The Yeomen of the Guard still conduct a mock search in the cellars of the building before the State opening of Parliament.

6

The bayberry is a New World plant. Bayberry-scented candles are an American tradition.

7

Hopscotch was played by children on north English roads when Britain was a Roman province. A hopscotch court was found scratched on some paving stones in a Roman excavation there.

8

To preserve Potatoes from the Frost

If you have not a convenient store-place for them, dig a trench three or four feet deep, into which they are to be laid as they are taken up, and then covered with the earth taken out of the trench, raised up in the middle like the roof of a house, and covered with straw to carry off the rain. They will be thus preserved from the frost, and can be taken up as they are wanted.

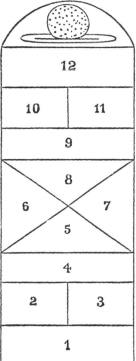

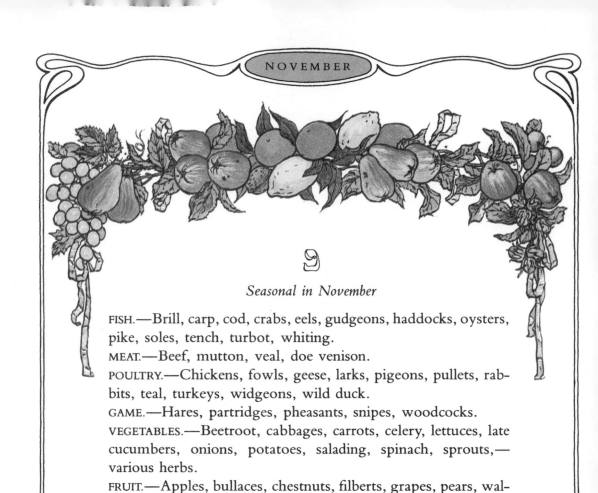

9

Seasonal in November

FISH.—Brill, carp, cod, crabs, eels, gudgeons, haddocks, oysters, pike, soles, tench, turbot, whiting.

MEAT.—Beef, mutton, veal, doe venison.

POULTRY.—Chickens, fowls, geese, larks, pigeons, pullets, rabbits, teal, turkeys, widgeons, wild duck.

GAME.—Hares, partridges, pheasants, snipes, woodcocks.

VEGETABLES.—Beetroot, cabbages, carrots, celery, lettuces, late cucumbers, onions, potatoes, salading, spinach, sprouts,—various herbs.

FRUIT.—Apples, bullaces, chestnuts, filberts, grapes, pears, walnuts.

10

> If you wed in bleak November,
> Only joys will come, remember.

11

St. Menas' Day in Greece. He is believed to be able to locate lost belongings, especially sheep.

The trumpet of a prophecy! O Wind,
If Winter comes, can Spring be far behind?
Shelley

12

St. Martin's Day, or Martinmas. He is the patron saint of tavern keepers, beggars, wine-growers, and drunkards. According to tradition, St. Martin hid in a barn because he didn't want to be made a bishop, but a goose gave his presence away. In many parts of Europe, roast goose is eaten on this day.

To make Starch Molds and Cast Candies

Fill a box-cover with corn-starch, having it very light and dry; shake it down even. Press into it a die of any shape desired, making the indentations carefully. A smooth flat button one half inch in diameter makes a good shape for peppermints. Molds are used for cream drops, chocolates, or any of the flavored clear candies.

The liquid candy is dropped carefully into the molds and removed when cold and the starch dusted off. The starch can then be stirred light and again pressed into molds.

First flying trapeze act performed in 1859 by Jules Leotard at the Cirque Napoléon, Paris.

13

Robert Louis Stevenson born, 1850.

14

Hoop rolling used to be a boys' game, and teams of boys would have hoop wars; the object was to run hoops past the enemy's lines.

Now flies the ball, now rolls the whirling hoop.

Ovid, Tristia

15

Seven-Five-Three Festival Day in Japan: Parents give thanks for the wellbeing of girls aged seven and three, boys aged five and three.

16

At London's Guildhall in 1848, the last public performance by Chopin.

17

Day of St. Hilda, patroness of business and professional women.

November take flaile,
Let ship no more saile.

In the 1840s there was a craze in England for building and investing in railroads. An Act of Parliament decreed that plans for any railway scheme had to be deposited by this date in 1845. On the last day, promoters raced to get their papers in; 28 express trains were chartered just for that purpose, and in one instance two of them collided. Plans for 620 schemes were filed, 272 became Acts of Parliament—only to collapse later.

November.

1 22 S. AFT. TRIN.
2 Monday.
3 Tuesday.
4 Wednesday.
5 Thursday.
6 Friday.
7 Saturday.
8 23 S. AFT. TRIN.
9 Monday.
10 Tuesday.
11 Wednesday.
12 Thursday.
13 Friday.
14 Saturday.
15 24 S. AFT. TRIN.
16 Monday.
17 Tuesday.
18 Wednesday.
19 Thursday.
20 Friday.
21 Saturday.
22 25 S. AFT. TRIN.
23 Monday.
24 Tuesday.
25 Wednesday.
26 Thursday.
27 Friday.
28 Saturday.
29 1 SUN. IN ADV.
30 Monday.

New Moon.
6th day, 9 h. 3 m. aftern.
First Quarter.
14th day, 10 h. 0 m. aftern.
Full Moon.
22nd day, 9 h. 39 m. morn.
Last Quarter.
29th day, 1 h. 57 m. morn.

18

19

When cold weather comes, we look for indoor pastimes. The first ping-pong set was improvised in the 1880s by James Gibb, a British engineer and athlete, whose family played the game on their dining-room table, using cigar-box lids for paddles and balls made from champagne corks.

20

Girls begin playing jacks when the weather gets cold and they have to spend more time indoors. Aristophanes mentions this game—it was called "five-stones". Five pebbles or bones were tossed up and caught on the back of the hand; any that fell to the ground had to be picked up with the fingers while the others remained on the hand.

21

The phonograph is invented by Thomas Edison, 1877.

22

SAGITTARIUS   ♐   *The Archer.*

The sun enters the ninth zodiac sign of the year, Sagittarius.

Legend has it that Robin Hood lived in the time of Edward II. In the royal household expense records there is said to be an entry under 22 Nov. 1324: "To Robin Hood, by command, owing to his being unable any longer to work, the sum of 5s". According to the story, Edward befriended Robin Hood after the latter captured him, disguised as a monk, in Sherwood Forest.

St. Cecilia's Day. She is the patron saint of music, singers, and poets.

23

Burn an orange peel on the stove to cover annoying cooking smells.

The chimney all sootie would now be made cleene,
    for feare of mischances, too oftentimes seene:
Old chimney and sootie, if fire once take,
    by burning and breaking, soon mischief may make.

24

*Thieves' Vinegar,
Reckoned an Excellent
Preservative Against Infection*

Take an ounce of the tops of wormwood; rosemary, sage, mint, and rue, of each half an ounce; flowers of lavender, two ounces; aromatic gum, cinnamon, cloves, nutmegs, and fresh garlic, two drachms of each; half an ounce of camphor, and eight pounds of red vinegar; beat all the ingredients well, put them into a proper earthen jar, and pour the vinegar upon them; the garlic ought to be sliced. After stopping the jar, put it in the sun or in a hot place, such as a sand bath, for three or four weeks; wring out the ingredients, and filter it through grey paper; the camphor must be dissolved in a little spirits of wine. This vinegar ought to be kept closely corked.

November.

1 Thursday.	11 24 S. AF.TRI.	21 Wednesday.
2 Friday.	12 Monday.	22 Thursday.
3 Saturday.	13 Tuesday.	23 Friday.
4 23 S AF.TRI.	14 Wednesday	24 Saturday.
5 Monday.	15 Thursday.	25 26 S. AF.TRI.
6 Tuesday.	16 Friday.	26 Monday.
7 Wednesday.	17 Saturday.	27 Tuesday.
8 Thursday.	18 25 S. AF.TRI	28 Wednesday.
9 Friday.	19 Monday.	29 Thursday.
10 Saturday.	20 Tuesday.	30 St. And. Day.

25

In 1834, a full meal at a fine New York hotel costs 12 cents.

26

The opening of Tutankhamen's tomb, Egypt, 1922.

New World's first tramway begins operation. New York, 1832.

At Ashburton, Devon, the following offices were filled on this date for over 1000 years: Ale Tasters, Bread Weighers, Pig Drivers, Scavengers, Surveyors of Markets and Water Courses, Portreeve. The latter office (the Mayor) continues to this day.

27

NOVEMBER.

1. Thursday.	16. Friday.
2. Friday.	17. Saturday.
3. Saturday.	18. SUNDAY.
4. SUNDAY.	19. Monday.
5. Monday.	20. Tuesday.
6. Tuesday.	21. Wednesday.
7. Wednesday.	22. Thursday.
8. Thursday.	23. Friday.
9. Friday.	24. Saturday.
10. Saturday.	25. SUNDAY.
11. SUNDAY.	26. Monday.
12. Monday.	27. Tuesday.
13. Tuesday.	28. Wednesday.
14. Wednesday.	29. Thursday.
15. Thursday.	30. Friday.

THANKSGIVING

In America, children used to go around begging in disguise at Thanksgiving time.

The turkey was a New World bird, discovered by the Spanish conquistadores about 1518. Some say it got its name because it seemed exotic, the way Turkey seemed exotic to Europeans of that time.

In 1863, Abraham Lincoln proclaimed a Thanksgiving holiday on the last Thursday in November. Franklin Delano Roosevelt changed it to the next-to-last Thursday.

The first Thanksgiving was in 1621, when the smell of roasting turkeys drew ninety friendly Indians to share in the settlers' harvest celebration. The fifty-five English participants included only four women, who did all the cooking.

Alfred Nobel's will establishes
the Nobel Foundation, 1896.

28

In 1893, women vote in a national election for the first time—in the New Zealand General Elections.

Shakespeare and Anne Hathaway marry, 1582.

29

Louisa May Alcott born, 1832.

30

Day of St. Andrew, patron saint of Scotland, Greece, fishermen, and golfers.

Samuel Clemens (Mark Twain) born, 1835.

At Eton, an ancient and mysterious game called the Eton Wall Game is played. The goals on the field are a chalk mark on a wall and a mark on a tree. Most of the game consists of scrimmages against the wall and there is seldom a score.

ADVENT

Advent includes the four Sundays before Christmas, beginning with the one nearest November 30th. In Normandy at this time, farmers used to send children with torches into the fields to exorcise them. The youngsters would burn bundles of hay and cry:

> Mice, caterpillars, and moles;
> Get out, get out of my field;
> I will burn your beard and bones;
>   Trees and shrubs
>   Give me bushels of apples.

DÉ CEM BRE

DECEMBER

December.

1	Monday	12	Friday	23	Tuesday
2	Tuesday	13	Saturday	24	Wednesday
3	Wednesday	14	3 S. in Adv.	25	*Christms. D.*
4	Thursday	15	Monday	26	Bank Holid.
5	Friday	16	Tuesday	27	Saturday
6	Saturday	17	Wednesday	28	1 S. af. Chr.
7	2 S. in Adv.	18	Thursday	29	Monday
8	Monday	19	Friday	30	Tuesday
9	Tuesday	20	Saturday	31	Wednesday
10	Wednesday	21	4 S. in Adv.		
11	Thursday	22	Monday		

We shall hear
The rain and wind beat dark December.
Shakespeare, Cymbeline

1

December is the tenth month of the old Roman calendar. The Saxons called it *Winter Monath* and, after the conversion to Christianity, *Heligh Monath*—Holy month.

2

Sleds—which later developed into sleighs on runners—were the first vehicles. They were used before the wheel was invented.

3

HANNUKAH

The Jewish feast of lights commemorates the overcoming of the Syrian hordes by Judas Maccabeus. The candle-lighting ceremony recalls the rekindling of lights in the Temple after it was recaptured. It is said that a lamp holding one day's supply of oil burned for eight days.

4

Richfield Springs, New York: Delina Filkins dies in 1928 at the age of 113 years 7 months, the oldest human being that ever lived, as proven by documents. Some dispute the proof and claim the record for the Canadian Pierre Joubert, who died in 1814 at 113 years 4 months.

In the Middle Ages, a liquid called *posset* was drunk alone and used in cooking. It was made of milk mixed with ale, or wine, and spices, and heated.

5

Columbus establishes the first New World settlement in St. Domingo, 1492.

6

ST. NICHOLAS' DAY

Before the Reformation it was common throughout England to elect a boy bishop on St. Nicholas' Day. He would exercise jurisdiction until Innocents', or Childermas Day (December 28), and was entitled to a monument and burial as a bishop if he died during his tenure. At least one King of England heard the mass celebrated by a boy bishop.

St. Nicholas was supposedly so devout he did not even suck on the fast days of Wednesday and Friday. He is the patron saint of Russia, and the special guardian of virgins, children, sailors, scholars, and robbers. Three bags of gold he once supplied as doweries to an impoverished family became the three-ball symbol of the pawnbroker.

In France, the Bonhomme Noël leaves presents on the hearth on St. Nicholas' Eve. Also, Père Noël and his companion Père Fouettard, who knows how children have behaved all year, come on either December 6 or December 24.

The sun, that brief December day,
Rose cheerless over hills of gray,
And, darkly circled, gave at noon
A sadder light than waning moon.
J. G. Whittier

In a 1660 London performance of Shakespeare's *Othello,* Desdemona is played by a woman; the first time in England a woman plays a part of some importance on the stage.

December.

1 Tuesday.
2 Wednesday.
3 Thursday.
4 Friday.
5 Saturday.
6 2 SUN. IN ADV.
7 Monday.
8 Tuesday.
9 Wednesday.
10 Thursday.
11 Friday.
12 Saturday.
13 3 SUN. IN ADV
14 Monday.
15 Tuesday.
16 Wednesday.
17 Thursday.
18 Friday.
19 Saturday.
20 4 SUN. IN ADV.
21 Monday.
22 Tuesday.
23 Wednesday.
24 Thursday.
25 *Christmas Day.*
26 Bank Holiday.
27 1 S. AFT. CHRIS.
28 Monday.
29 Tuesday.
30 Wednesday.
31 Thursday.

New Moon.
6th day, 1 h. 17 m. aftern.
First Quarter.
14th day, 6 h. 22 m. aftern.
Full Moon.
21st day, 8 h. 59 m. aftern.
Last Quarter.
28th day, o h. 22 m. aftern.

House sparrows are one of the few birds that do not go South in Winter. They were brought to New York in 1850, supposedly by someone who wanted to bring to the United States every species of bird mentioned in Shakespeare's plays.

As winter approaches, it is impossible to be too careful in keeping spare beds and blankets properly aired. In damp weather, a bed which has been unoccupied for three successive nights, is unfit for the use of a delicate person, or, indeed, of anyone; if they cannot be put under the occupied beds of the house, a cleanly servant should sleep in them alternately.

Blow, blow, thou winter wind,
Thou art not so unkind
  As man's ingratitude;
Thy tooth is not so keen,
Because thou art not seen,
  Although thy breath be rude.
Heigh-ho! sing, heigh-ho! unto the green holly:
Most friendship is feigning, most loving mere folly:
Then, heigh-ho, the holly!
  This life is most jolly.

Shakespeare, As You Like It

10

Announced by all the trumpets of the sky,
Arrives the snow, and, driving o'er the fields,
Seems nowhere to alight: the whited air
Hides hills and woods, the river, and the heaven,
And veils the farmhouse at the garden's end.
The sled and traveler stopped, the courier's feet
Delayed, all friends shut out, the housemates sit
Around the radiant fireplace, enclosed
In a tumultuous privacy of storm.

Emerson

11

Christmas is coming, the geese are getting fat,
Please to put a penny in an old man's hat;
If you haven't a penny, a ha' penny will do,
If you haven't got a ha' penny, God bless you.

12

Panada is a simple dish for sick people; it appears over and over in the 19th century cookbooks. Put a crumbled soda cracker in a small bowl of boiling water with two or three lumps of sugar and grate a little fresh nutmeg over it.

13

The Day of St. Lucia; a feast of lights in Sweden. No one knows who the real St. Lucia was, but on this morning—the darkest day of the year in Sweden—the oldest daughter of the family goes to wake her parents, wearing a crown of pine boughs decorated with lighted candles.

Ice cream mold patented by Italo Marcioni, New Jersey, 1904.

14

A "Lyon of Barbary" was displayed in Boston in 1716. In December 1733, a "Fine Large White Bear" from Greenland was exhibited there and was declared by one of those who had seen the "Lyon" to be "a sight far preferable".

15

For writing Christmas cards

Red Ink

Take a quarter of a pound of the best Brazil wood (get it in the log if possible, and rasp or shave it yourself), one ounce of cream of tartar, and one ounce of alum; boil these ingredients in a quart of clear water till half is consumed, then add to the ink, when filtered hot, one ounce of gum-arabic and one ounce of fine sugar. A little salt added will prevent it from becoming mouldy.

16

The Boston Tea Party, 1773.

17

A Christmas Carol by Dickens published, 1843.

Beginning of the Saturnalia, a week-long festival in ancient Rome. The social order was reversed, slaves were waited upon by their masters, whom they were free to insult. All business was stopped, and the whole week was devoted to feasting and gambling.

Our year-end week of festivities goes back to this Roman custom which it resembles in many ways. The Romans decorated their houses with laurel branches and lit them with candles to ward off the spirits of darkness—this being the darkest time of the year. They also gave gifts: preserved fruits, cakes, candles, frankincense, and objects of clay, gold, and silver.

The Wright brothers fly their machine for 12 seconds at Kitty Hawk in 1903. Man's first successful propelled flight.

In the Middle Ages, a Lord of Misrule was appointed during this week. He was also called the Master of Merry Disports, and led the revels at Christmas festivals in the Court and colleges. Upon taking office, he absolved everyone of their wisdom, and conducted wild, expensive revels which incurred the displeasure of the Puritans.

At this time of the year in Northern Europe, Yule logs were burned in honor of Odin and Thor. The word "yule" comes from *Jul,* the ancient name of the Thor festival, now Swedish for Christmas.

DECEMBER.

1. Saturday.	16. Sunday.
2. Advent Sunday.	17. Monday.
3. Monday.	18. Tuesday.
4. Tuesday.	19. Wednesday.
5. Wednesday.	20. Thursday.
6. Thursday.	21. Friday.
7. Friday.	22. Saturday.
8. Saturday.	23. Sunday.
9. Sunday.	24. Monday.
10. Monday.	25. Christmas Day.
11. Tuesday.	26. Wednesday.
12. Wednesday.	27. Thursday.
13. Thursday.	28. Friday.
14. Friday.	29. Saturday.
15. Saturday.	30. Sunday.
	31. Monday.

18

In the Middle Ages, cooks colored foods with dyes made by boiling herbs or flowers in wine:

    for green—parsley or mint
    for blue—heliotrope
    for red or pink—sandalwood.

19

For coughs: one teaspoonful to one tablespoonful of a syrup made of equal parts of edible linseed oil (not the kind used for furniture polish), good rum, and honey.

20

A flying machine is invented in 1709 by a Brazilian priest. According to a newspaper, it ran by a combination of wind power, magnetism, and amber beads "which by a Secret Operation will help to keep the Ship Aloft".

WINTER

WINTER.

Winter tames man, woman and beast.

Shakespeare, The Taming of the Shrew

21

St. Thomas's Day. This being the time of the winter solstice, an old rhyme goes:

> St. Thomas Grey, St. Thomas Grey,
> The longest night and the shortest day.

The first crossword puzzle appears; in the New York *World,* 1913.

In 1825, a Munich innkeeper sponsored a dumpling-eating contest with prizes. The victor ate 38 in one hour; a total of 2642 were consumed (Bavarian dumplings—*Knödel*—are about the size of a small melon).

December.

1 Saturday.	11 Tuesday.	22 Saturday.
2 ADVENT SY.	12 Wednesday.	23 4 S.IN ADVN.
3 Monday.	13 Thursday.	24 Monday.
4 Tuesday.	14 Friday.	25 Christmas D.
5 Wednesday.	15 Saturday.	26 Bank Holid.
6 Thursday.	16 3 S.IN ADVN.	27 Thursday.
7 Friday.	17 Monday.	28 Friday.
8 Saturday.	18 Tuesday.	29 Saturday.
9 2 S.IN ADVN.	19 Wednesday.	30 1 S. AFT. CH.
10 Monday.	20 Thursday.	31 Monday.
	21 Friday.	

22

When December snows fall fast,
Marry, and true love will last.

Cleave logs now all,
for kitchen and hall.

23

CAPRICORNUS   ♑   *The Goat.*

The sun enters the tenth zodiac sign of the year, Capricorn.

24

God bless the master of this house,
    The mistress bless also,
And all the little children
    That round the table go;
And all your kin and kinsmen,
    That dwell both far and near,
I wish you a merry Christmas,
    And a happy new year.

In the Middle Ages, a carol was not a song but a ring dance, danced by the family at Christmas time around the crib of a baby.

Some believed that on Christmas Eve: Animals have the gift of speech, cattle bow to the East, bees hum the 100th Psalm in their hives.

The Yule log is an emblem of good luck. It should be only half-burnt, the remainder kept to light the new log on next Christmas Eve. It is bad luck if a squinty or barefoot person, or a flat-footed woman, enters the house while the fire is burning.

CHRISTMAS

At Christmas we banquet the rich with the poore,
Who then (but the miser) but openeth his doore?

The first Christmas tree was described in 1605 by a visitor to Strasbourg, who wrote: "For Christmas they have fir-trees in their rooms, all decorated with paper roses, apples, sugar, gold and wafers".

You are supposed to make a wish when you stir a plum pudding.

In the Middle Ages, the traditional roast boar served at Christmas had rosemary in its ears to represent the returning summer, and a piece of fruit in its mouth to represent the sun at the darkest time of the year.

Boar's head with mustard was the most popular traditional Christmas dish, but it didn't survive the efforts of the Puritans to repress Christmas. Mince-pie and plum pudding are traditional dishes which are still eaten. One delicacy considered indispensable in early times—furmante (also known as frumenty or furmety)—is no longer around. It was a concoction of hulled and soaked wheat, "tempered" with almond milk and egg yolks, with sugar added.

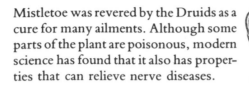

Mistletoe was revered by the Druids as a cure for many ailments. Although some parts of the plant are poisonous, modern science has found that it also has properties that can relieve nerve diseases.

Goose is eaten at Christmas-time in France. It is believed that a goose was there to welcome the Three Wise Men.

The Romans called this day, when the sun was weakest by their calendar, *Dies Natalis Invicti Solis*—Birthday of the Unconquered Sun.

Blindman's buff is a traditional Christmas-time game.

In Scandinavia, it is said that Christmas gifts come from gnomes who live in the attics of houses all year round.

It is a Dutch custom to go to great lengths to disguise Christmas presents; people will go so far as to wrap a package, then coat it with dough and bake it in the oven to make it look like a bread.

Card-playing used to be a Christmas custom; people who otherwise never played would do so at Christmas-time. Sir Roger de Coverley would send "a string of hog's pudding and a pack of cards" to every poor family in the parish.

26

Boxing Day in Britain was originally a day when servants carried boxes around to collect bonuses from their employers; more recently, a day when holiday gifts are given to service people.

27

All Fool's Day in Mexico. Things borrowed on this day need not be returned; instead, the lender is sent a poem telling him he is a fool.

A medieval feast specialty was a peacock from which the skin was removed with the feathers still in, and then put back on the peacock after the meat had been roasted; the re-feathered, cooked peacock, with its bill and claws gilded, was brought to the table looking like a live bird.

28

Mummers were masked actors who played out the story of St. George. Some of the characters were: The dragon, The Grand Turk, a pretty girl, and a doctor, with pills to treat the wounded.

The gifts of frankincense and myrrh were as precious as gold in biblical times. Frankincense is a resin with a strong scent of balsam that was used by the ancients for embalming. Myrrh is also an aromatic resin prized as a perfume, a spice, and a medicine. It was once worn on the crowns of Persian kings to symbolize wealth.

MYRRH

29

Good bread and good drink, a good fire in the hall
Brawn, pudding, and pigs' feet, and good mustard withall.

30

The New Year's season is known in Scotland as the Daft Days. New Year's Eve itself is known as Hogmanay, but the origins of this term are unclear. A mysterious feature of Hogmanay is the parading of mummers, known as "guisers", or "guizards", attended by boys dressed up as an old woman, known as Bessie.

The first public concert was held in London in 1672. One shilling admission was charged, and patrons could order ale and cakes while they listened to musicians performing behind a curtain.

31

At midnight on December 31, it is customary to unbar the house-door when the hour has struck, to "let out the Old, and let in the New Year".

JANVIER

JANUARY

January.

1	Wednesday	17	Friday
2	Thursday	18	Saturday
3	Friday	19	2 S. AF. EPH.
4	Saturday	20	Monday
5	2 S. AF. CHR.	21	Tuesday
6	EPIPHANY	22	Wednesday
7	Tuesday	23	Thursday
8	Wednesday	24	Friday
9	Thursday	25	Saturday
10	Friday	26	3 S. AF. EPH.
11	Saturday	27	Monday
12	1 S. AF. EPH.	28	Tuesday
13	Monday	29	Wednesday
14	Tuesday	30	Thursday
15	Wednesday	31	Friday
16	Thursday		

Pale January lay
In its cradle day by day,
Dead or living, hard to say.
Alfred Austin

1

NEW YEAR'S DAY

In the old Roman calendar, in the days of the republic, the year began on March 1 and ended on December 31. January and February were added later.

In the old days on festive occasions, by English tradition the family would drink "lamb's wool"—a spiced ale—saying, in Saxon, *Wass hael:* To your health. The bowl from which they drank became known as the Wassail Bowl.

Wassail, wassail, to our town,
The cup is white, the ale is brown:
The cup is made of the ashen tree,
And so is the ale of the good barley.

Little maid, pretty maid, turn the pin,
Open the door and let us come in:
God be here, God be there,
I wish you all a Happy New Year.

It used to be the custom to exchange gifts on New Year's Day. Gloves were often given, or else the money to purchase them, which was known as "glove money". This custom was extended to metal pins, introduced in the 16th century. Eventually, "pin money" came to mean the money set aside by a husband for his wife's expenditures.

In most European countries people call on each other on New Year's Day, bringing gifts of food and drink. In many places it is believed that the first person to enter a house after the New Year determines what kind of year it will be. In some parts of Britain, people hope that the first person to cross their doorstep in the New Year will be a dark-haired man, because this brings good luck.

The Hebrew New Year of Trees occurs around this time. People used to plant a cedar when a boy was born, a cypress for a girl, and use the grown trees for wedding canopies when the children married.

In the Middle Ages, feasting at New Year's and other times was justified by the idea that occasional excess helped people achieve self-control at other times.

Who dainties love,
a beggar shall prove.

In Rio de Janeiro, thousands of candles burn on beaches in honor of the Sea Queen. Women in white robes cast flower petals into the water.

Since the time of Henry IV, it had been customary to present New Year's gifts to rulers. The custom reached its height under Queen Elizabeth, who received as a gift in 1561 her first pair of silk stockings and foreswore woolen and cotton hose forever.

President Theodore Roosevelt shakes 8513 Happy New Year hands, a record. 1907.

The first train in Africa, 1856, between Alexandria and Cairo.

It was a very old belief that for a happy year you had to eat mince pie on all the twelve days of Christmas.

In Spain and Portugal, New Year's celebrants eat a grape for each chime of the clock at midnight.

The serving of coffee on New Year's Day is an old American custom.

Coffee is considered beneficial to rheumatic persons, in which case it is usual to stir in a little made mustard.

> *To make Coffee as used by Buonaparte.*
>
> Put the ground coffee into a vessel with a strainer, and pour the water on it perfectly cold; plunge this vessel into another filled with boiling water, which must be kept at the boiling pitch till the process is completed. This method is thought to preserve the flavour, of the coffee.

In the medieval monasteries, acorns were ground to make a coffee-like drink.

2

Day of St. Macarius, patron saint of confectioners.

Work Day in Japan—a good day for beginning work.

3

J. R. R. Tolkien born, 1892.

Paper drinking straws are patented, 1888.

4

January is a depressing time of year for many people. In the Middle Ages, people with melancholy dispositions were advised to avoid fried meats and overly salty foods. Venison was believed to engender melancholy.

5

The first Monday of the year is known in Scotland as Handsel Monday, a handsel being the Scottish equivalent of the box used by the English on Boxing Day. Traditionally, workmen are given tips on this day, and it is the day old servants leave and new ones are hired. When the calendar changed in 1752, the day was moved to the first Monday after January 12, but many still keep the old date.

6

EPIPHANY

TWELFTH DAY

The twelfth day after Christmas was the day when the Wise Men arrived to see the infant Jesus. In Spain, children receive their gifts from the Wise Men; they leave their shoes on their windowsills full of straw for the Wise Men's mounts.

It is bad luck to take down your Christmas decorations before Twelfth Night.

At Christmas-time in Greece, celebrated on Twelfth Day, people keep basil sprigs and a cross in a glass of water to keep away the *kalikangare*—goblins from the center of the earth said to roam the world at this season.

7

St. Distaff's Day. There was no such person as St. Distaff—the distaff is the spindle on a spinning wheel and the housewife was supposed to go back to her usual routines on this day after the holiday season—the name of the day is a medieval joke.

Bid Christmas adiew, thy stock now renew.

8

In Italy, an old woman called Befana (from Epiphania) brings children their presents. It is believed that she started out a day too late to look for the infant Jesus after the Wise Men passed her door, and has been traveling around looking for him ever since.

To clean carpets: Sprinkle with wet tea leaves, sweep them up, then use soap and warm water.

9

Now season is good, to lop or fell wood.

10

Holiday feasting always brings spills and stains.

To take the Stains of Grease from Woollen or Silk.

Three ounces of spirits of wine, three ounces of French chalk, powdered, and five ounces of pipe-clay. Mix the above ingredients, and make them up in rolls about the length of a finger, and you will find a never-failing remedy for removing grease from woollen or silken goods.

N. B.—It is to be applied by rubbing on the spot either dry or wet, and afterwards brushing the place.

11

Holland is the birthplace of the now popular winter sport, ice skating. Ice skates were originally made with the leg-bones of animals.

In an Amsterdam church filled to capacity, Jan. J. Mauricius preaches for one hour—he is 6½ years old. 1699.

12

Dove house repaire,
make dovehole faire.

13

The 1752 Act changing the start of the British legal year from March 25 to January 1. The calendar was adjusted by making the day after September 3 the 14th. Segments of the English population were outraged, demanding of the politicians, "Who stole the eleven days? Give us back the eleven days!"

Horatio Alger born, 1832.

JANUARY.

1. Monday.	16. Tuesday.
2. Tuesday.	17. Wednesday.
3. Wednesday.	18. Thursday.
4. Thursday.	19. Friday.
5. Friday.	20. Saturday.
6. Saturday.	21. Sunday.
7. Sunday.	22. Monday,
8. Monday.	23. Tuesday.
9. Tuesday.	24. Wednesday.
10. Wednesday.	25. Thursday.
11. Thursday.	26. Friday.
12. Friday.	27. Saturday.
13. Saturday.	28. Sunday.
14. Sunday.	29. Monday.
15. Monday.	30. Tuesday.
	31. Wednesday.

14

The names of some popular 18th century New England dances: Old Father George, Cape Breton, High Betty Martin, Assembly, The President, Pettycoatee, The Lady's Choice, Rolling Hornpipe, Constancy, Orange Tree, Springfield, Miss Foster's Delight, Priest's House, Leather the Strap.

15

Calves likely that come between Christmas and Lent,
take housewife to rear, or else after repent.

(Any calf born between Christmas and Lent should be raised
by hand by the farmer's wife, or it won't survive.)

16

In the cold winter of 1649, John Evelyn walks on the frozen
Thames from Westminster to Lambeth to dine with the arch-
bishop of Canterbury. He notes that there are shops on the ice,
even a printing press where one may order paper with one's
name, the date, and the address "the Thames" printed on it.

17

January.

1 Thursday.
2 Friday.
3 Saturday.
4 2 S. AFT. CHRIS.
5 Monday.
6 Epiphany.
7 Wednesday.
8 Thursday.
9 Friday.
10 Saturday.
11 1 S. AFT. EPIP.
12 Monday.
13 Tuesday.
14 Wednesday.
15 Thursday.
16 Friday.
17 Saturday.
18 2 S. AFT. EPIP.
19 Monday.
20 Tuesday.
21 Wednesday.
22 Thursday.
23 Friday.
24 Saturday.
25 3 S. AFT. EPIP.
26 Monday.
27 Tuesday.
28 Wednesday.
29 Thursday.
30 Friday.
31 Saturday.

Last Quarter.
8th day, 3 h. 37 m. morn.
New Moon.
16th day, 8 h. 37 m. morn.
First Quarter.
24th day, 1 h. 26 m. morn.
Full Moon.
30th day, 4 h. 19 m. aftern.

Benjamin Franklin born, 1706.

With the old Almanack and the old year,
Leave thy old Vices, tho' ever so dear.

Benjamin Franklin

Twelfth Night according to very old calendars. In Devonshire and Cornwall there was the custom of wassailing the apple trees; in order to drive away evil spirits, men shot guns through the branches of the largest tree in the orchard, threw cider over its trunk, and put pieces of toast and cake in the crotch of its limbs.

18

According to legend, the game of badminton was invented in the 19th century by an English duke who wanted to play tennis indoors in his house in Badminton without hurting his art collection.

> Honey and vinegar, simmered together, have often been found beneficial in an asthmatic cough. Or the following:—Sugar-candy, bruised, oil of sweet almonds, and lemon-juice mixed together.

19

Freeze, freeze, thou bitter sky,
That dost not bite so nigh
    As benefits forgot:
Though thou the waters warp,
Thy sting is not so sharp
    As friend remembered not.
Heigh-ho! sing, . . .

Shakespeare, As You Like It

20

The first Parliament with the Commons (common people) represented, 1265. Although the nobles remained in firm control, this was the first time that the principle of popular representation was acknowledged.

St. Agnes' Eve. According to tradition, a girl who goes to sleep without supper will dream of the man she is to marry. Keats wrote:

    . . . upon St. Agnes's Eve
    Young virgins might have visions of delight . . .
    If ceremonies due they did aright.

21

AQUARIUS ≈ The Water-Bearer.

The sun enters the eleventh zodiac sign of the year, Aquarius.

22

Sauce for Larks

Larks; roast them, and for sauce have crumbs of bread, done thus; take a sauce-pan, or stew-pan, and some butter when melted, have a good piece of crumb of bread, and rub it in a clean cloth to crumbs, then throw into your pan; keep stirring them about till they are brown, then throw them into a sieve to drain and lay them round your larks.

23

Cement to mend broken China or Glass.

Garlic stamped in a stone mortar; the juice whereof, when applied to the pieces to be joined together, is the finest and strongest cement for that purpose, and will leave little or no mark if done with care.

24

In 1516, King Francis I of France visits the little island of If, near Marseilles. There he sees an Indian rhinoceros, on its way to the Pope—a gift from King Emanuel of Portugal. The animal never reached its destination because the ship in which it was sent was wrecked. It became famous, however, because of the engraving of it made by Dürer—who had never seen it or any other rhinocerous.

25

O Winter, king of intimate delights,
Fire-side enjoyments, home-born happiness,
And all the comforts that the lowly roof
Of undisturb'd retirement, and the hours
Of long uninterrupted ev'ning, know.

William Cowper

First Olympic winter games, Chamonix, 1924.

Conversion of St. Paul Day. In New York, the churchyard of St. Paul's chapel in the Wall Street area is closed for the two days before this day. According to law, if it is used uninterruptedly as a public passage for a year, the owners lose their rights to it.

26

At the premiere of Corneille's *Andromede* in Paris, a horse plays the part of Pegasus, the Winged Horse. This is the first known appearance of a living animal on stage. About 1650.

27

Lewis Carroll born, 1832.

In Puritan New England, babies were baptized on the first Sunday after birth—even if there was ice in the christening font.

28

St. Charlemagne's Day was celebrated by French students with champagne breakfasts. Although he could not read or write, the First Holy Roman Emperor is by tradition the founder of the University of Paris.

To take Wax out of Velvet of all Colours except Crimson.

Take a crummy wheaten loaf, cut it in two, toast it before the fire, and while very hot, apply it to the part spotted with wax. Then apply another piece of toasted bread hot as before, and continue this application till the wax is entirely taken out.

29

Owls mate in January, and their mating calls can be heard at this time of year. The owl's name apparently comes from its call—in Latin it was *ulula*, which became *ule* and then *owl*.

The Académie Française is founded by Richelieu, 1635.

Out of the bosom of the Air,
   Out of the cloud-folds of her garments shaken,
Over the woodlands brown and bare,
   Over the harvest-fields forsaken,
      Silent, and soft, and slow
      Descends the snow.   *Longfellow*

30

Young couples in early America had to do their winter courting sitting with everyone else in the only room with a fire, so they whispered to each other through five-foot-long hollow tubes.

31

At Guilford, in Surrey, two maidservants "not employed in beerhouses or hostelry" rolled dice for 11 pounds 19 shillings, the interest on a sum left for this purpose in a 1674 bequest.

FE
-VRI
-ER

FEBRUARY

February.

1	Saturday	15	Saturday
2	SEPTUAGES.	16	QUINQUA.
3	Monday	17	Monday
4	Tuesday	18	*Shrove Tues.*
5	Wednesday	19	*Ash Wednes.*
6	Thursday	20	Thursday
7	Friday	21	Friday
8	Saturday	22	Saturday
9	SEXAGESIMA	23	1 S. IN LENT
10	Monday	24	Monday
11	Tuesday	25	Tuesday
12	Wednesday	26	Wednesday
13	Thursday	27	Thursday
14	Friday	28	Friday

If February give much snow
A fine Summer it doth foreshow.

1

The Malagasy believe that if a child is born on the first day of February, its house will burn down, so the family builds a little hut, the mother takes the baby inside, father sets fire to the hut, and mother runs out with the baby—both screaming.

Roman King Numa Pompilius introduced the leap year, determining that February would have 30 days only one year out of four, 29 the other three. The month's present 29-day leap year length is due to Augustus, who wanted August, the month named after him, to be as long as the six 31-day months, and took a day from the month which could least spare it.

2

Alexander Selkirk, the real Robinson Crusoe, is rescued, 1709.

Candlemas. There is an old belief that all hibernating animals awake on Candlemas and come out to see if it is still winter. If the weather is clear, the animals will go back to sleep for forty more days of winter—so people would hope for Candlemas to be cloudy. The Germans believed that the badger came out to look for his shadow, and transferred this belief to the American groundhog when they went to the New World.

3

There is a bean-throwing ceremony in Japan to mark the end of winter.

4

A year of snow, a year of plenty.

5

The Chinese New Year is celebrated at the new moon between January 21 and February 19. It lasts for 14 days, until the full moon, and is celebrated with a festival of lanterns and the parade of the dragon.

6

Day of St. Dorothea, patroness of gardeners.

7

Charles Dickens born, 1812.

Queen Wilhelmina marries Prince Henry of Mecklenburg in 1901. The city of Amsterdam presents the royal couple with a gilded coach.

8

Narvik Sun Pageant Day—the return of the sun is celebrated at Narvik, in Norway.

One of the strongest earthquakes in England, 1750. An irresponsible prediction of an earthquake on April 5 threw London into a panic. Quacks sold earthquake pills and earthquake gowns—to be worn by ladies staying outdoors all night. On the eve of April 5 the roads out of London were jammed with carriages and fleeing people.

9

Day of St. Apollonia, patron of toothache sufferers.

10

Mid-winter is the time for pruning. Old-time farmers pruned larger trees in winter to get extra firewood.

11

English wig makers petition King George III in 1765, imploring relief as changing fashions (men were wearing their own hair) and French competition were ruining them.

12

Rain in February is as good as manure.

February.

1	SEXAGESIM.	15	1 S. IN LENT
2	Monday	16	Monday
3	Tuesday	17	Tuesday
4	Wednesday	18	Wednesday
5	Thursday	19	Thursday
6	Friday	20	Friday
7	Saturday	21	Saturday
8	QUINQUA.	22	2 S. IN LENT
9	Monday	23	Monday
10	SHROVE TU.	24	Tuesday
11	ASH WED.	25	Wednesday
12	Thursday	26	Thursday
13	Friday	27	Friday
14	Saturday	28	Saturday

13

For reading old love letters:

To revive old Writings which are almost defaced

Boil gall nuts in wine; then steep a sponge into the liquor, and pass it on the lines of the old writing: by this method the letters which were almost undecypherable will appear as fresh as if newly done.

14

ST. VALENTINE'S DAY

February.

1 SEPTUAG. SUN.
2 Monday.
3 Tuesday.
4 Wednesday.
5 Thursday.
6 Friday.
7 Saturday.
8 SEXAGES. SUN.
9 Monday.
10 Tuesday.
11 Wednesday.
12 Thursday.
13 Friday.
14 Saturday.
15 QUINQUA. SUN.
16 Monday.
17 Shrove Tuesday.
18 Ash Wednesday.
19 Thursday.
20 Friday.
21 Saturday.
22 1 SUN. IN LENT.
23 Monday.
24 Tuesday.
25 Wednesday.
26 Thursday.
27 Friday.
28 Saturday.

Last Quarter.
6th day, 10 h. 38 m. aftern.
New Moon.
15th day, 2 h. 22 m. morn.
First Quarter.
22nd day, 10 h. 31 m. morn.
Fu'l Moon.
29th day, 4 h. 0 m. morn.

The Roman Festival of the Lupercalia, ·held in the middle of February, was a romantic occasion and probably the origin of St. Valentine's Day. Boys would draw girls' names out of a box and be paired off accordingly for the coming year. In some Roman eras, "licentious games" were also part of the festivities. In the Middle Ages, the church tried to make St. Valentine's Day religious by having people draw *saints'* names out of the box, and emulate the saint in the coming year, but by the 16th century girls' names were in the boxes again.

No one knows what the original St. Valentine (of whom there were at least two) had to do with love and romance.

Before 1653, Valentine greetings had to be delivered by hand. The first mailboxes in Europe were erected in Paris in 1653, but they did not last long because messengers afraid of losing their jobs put mice in them.

According to a very old belief, birds begin mating on St. Valentine's Day.

15

The Hague, Peace Palace, 1922: First session of the Permanent Court of International Justice.

16

In one year the household of King Richard II of England used 132,000 eggs.

17

The egg of the emu, a six-foot tall Australian bird, is equal to a dozen chicken eggs, it weighs about 1½ pounds (682 gr) and requires ½ hour to boil hard. Cakes made with emu eggs are said to be heavenly.

18

The Monday before Lent is called Collop Monday, Lentsherd Night, and Dappy-door Night in England. In the 19th century, children would ring doorbells and run away, or tie a string to the door and pull it closed when someone came out.

19

SHROVE TUESDAY

Shrove Tuesday has various names, all related to foods given up during Lent: Pancake Tuesday, Carnival (*carne vale*—farewell to meat), Mardi Gras (which means Fat Tuesday), and Doughnut Tuesday (in the United States, people ate doughnuts instead of pancakes—both were made to use up the fats, butter, and eggs in the house).

To preserve eggs, bury them upright in salt.

At Olney, Buckinghamshire, a famous pancake race is run: Only women may enter, and they must all wear a skirt, apron, hat, and scarf. Each contestant carries a frying pan, and must toss a pancake in it three times as she runs from the market square to the church door. She receives a kiss from the bell-ringer when she arrives. A similar race is run in Liberal, Kansas.

 20

ASH WEDNESDAY
The first day of Lent.

The word "Lent" comes from Anglo-Saxon *lencten*—the time of year when the days are lengthening.

In the Middle Ages, the beaver's tail was considered to be "fish" rather than "flesh", and so it could be eaten on the fast days in Lent.

PISCES   ♓   *The Fishes.*

The sun enters the twelfth zodiac sign of the year, Pisces.

21

February.

1	Wednesday.	11 Saturday.	21 Tuesday.
2	Thursday.	12 QUINQUA. S.	22 Wednesday.
3	Friday.	13 Monday.	23 Thursday.
4	Saturday.	14 Shrove Tues.	24 Friday.
5	SEXAGES. S.	15 Ash Wednes.	25 Saturday.
6	Monday.	16 Thursday.	26 2 S.IN LENT.
7	Tuesday.	17 Friday.	27 Monday.
8	Wednesday.	18 Saturday.	28 Tuesday.
9	Thursday.	19 1 S.IN LENT.	29 Wednesday.
10	Friday.	20 Monday.	

All Nature seems at work. Slugs leave their lair—
The bees are stirring—birds are on the wing—
And Winter slumbering in the open air
Wears on his smiling face a dream of Spring!

Samuel Taylor Coleridge,
Lines Composed 21st February 1825

22

George Washington born, 1732.

23

After the Thirty Years' War, which drastically reduced the population of Europe, the council at Nuremburg proclaimed: ". . . henceforth, for the next ten years, each male citizen is permitted to marry two wives".

24

Oak logs will warm you well
    If they're old and dry.
Larch logs of pinewood smell
    But the sparks will fly.
Beech logs for Christmas time,
    Yew logs heat well.
Scotch logs it is a crime
    For anyone to sell.
Birch logs burn too fast,
    Chestnut scarce at all.
Hawthorn logs are good to last
    If you cut them in the fall.

Holly logs will burn like wax,
    You should burn them green.
Elm logs like smouldering flax,
    No flame to be seen.
Pear logs and apple logs,
    They will scent your room.
Cherry logs across the dogs
    Smell like flowers in bloom.
But ash logs, all smooth and gray,
    Burn them green or old;
Buy up all that come your way,
    They're worth their weight in gold.

25

Artificial Ass's Milk

Mix two spoonfuls of boiling water, the same of milk, and an egg well beaten; sweeten with pounded white sugar-candy.

26

When February birds do mate,
You wed nor dread your fate.

27

For a dry tickling Cough

One ounce of spermaceti in powder, one table-spoonful of honey, a table-spoonful of simple peppermint-water, and the yolk of a new-laid egg; beat these up together, and take a spoonful often.

FEBRUARY.

1. Thursday.	15. Thursday.
2. Friday.	16. Friday.
3. Saturday.	17. Saturday.
4. Sunday.	18. Sunday.
5. Monday.	19. Monday.
6. Tuesday.	20. Tuesday.
7. Wednesday.	21. Wednesday.
8. Thursday.	22. Thursday.
9. Friday.	23. Friday.
10. Saturday.	24. Saturday.
11. Sunday.	25. Sunday.
12. Monday.	26. Monday.
13. Tuesday.	27. Tuesday.
14. Wednesday.	28. Wednesday.

28

John Tenniel born, 1820.

29

LEAP YEAR DAY

St. Bridget complained to St. Patrick that women could not propose marriage, so he permitted them to have this privilege on one day in one year out of four. When St. Bridget proposed to him, however, he turned her down and gave her a silk gown as a consolation present. Until the 19th century in Britain, a man was obliged to give a silk gown to any lady whose marriage proposal he refused in Leap Year.

This is the fifth Sunday of February, 1880. The occurrence of five Sundays in February comes only three times in a hundred years.